Elyse Fitzpatrick is one of the best authors you could read today if you want help truly loving Jesus and recognizing the deception of your own sinful heart that so easily leads you away from Him and back to your own patterns of self-destructive sin. Her book, 'Idols of the Heart' was one of the first to help us recognize the sin beneath the sin that so often goes undetected and leaves us confused. I'm thrilled that after fifteen years a second edition of this excellent work is now available. Elyse loves Jesus, she loves grace, and she loves helping people experience the freedom of truly loving Jesus with all their heart, and mind, and soul. This book can help you discover what may be keeping you from experiencing the fullness of His love.

—BRAD BIGNEY, Author, *Gospel Treason*

If you are struggling with desires, addictions, and harmful behaviors that seem too strong to overcome, perhaps you are worshipping an idol of the heart. Fitzpatrick explains what those idols might be and how to deal with them in a biblical way. *Idols of the Heart* is not just another self-help manual.

—ED BULKLEY, President, The International
Association of Biblical Counselors

Elyse Fitzpatrick has a very high view of God, and this book reflects that view. With great clarity and intriguing biblical illustrations, Elyse explains how the idols in our hearts compete with our affections for God. In a gentle way, she tells you how by God's grace to turn from your idols to a wholehearted love for God.

—MARTHA PEACE, Biblical Counselor; Author,
The Excellent Wife

The first and greatest commandment says that our relationship with God is a 'heart, soul, mind, and might' matter. God-substitutes,

IDOLS
of the
HEART

REVISED AND UPDATED

Learning to Long
for God Alone

ELYSE M. FITZPATRICK

PUBLISHING
P.O. BOX 817 • PHILLIPSBURG • NEW JERSEY 08865-0817

Unless otherwise indicated, Scripture quotations are from the NEW AMERICAN STANDARD BIBLE®. ©Copyright The Lockman Foundation 1960, 1962, 1963, 1968, 1971, 1972, 1973, 1975, 1977, 1995. Used by permission.

Scripture quotations marked ESV are from the ESV® Bible (*The Holy Bible, English Standard Version®*), copyright © 2001 by Crossway, a publishing ministry of Good News Publishers. Used by permission. All rights reserved.

Scripture quotations marked TLB are taken from The Living Bible, copyright © 1971 by Tyndale House Publishers, Wheaton, Illinois. Used by permission.

Scripture quotations marked KJV are from the King James Version.

Scripture quotations marked NIV are from the HOLY BIBLE, NEW INTERNATIONAL VERSION®. NIV®. Copyright © 1973, 1978, 1984 by International Bible Society. Used by permission of Zondervan Publishing House. All rights reserved.

Scripture quotations marked NKJV are from The Holy Bible, New King James Version. Copyright © 1979, 1980, 1982, Thomas Nelson, Inc.

Italics in Scripture quotations indicate emphasis added.

ISBN: 978-1-62995-210-9 (pbk)
ISBN: 978-1-62995-211-6 (ePub)
ISBN: 978-1-62995-212-3 (Mobi)

Printed in the United States of America

Library of Congress Cataloging-in-Publication Data

Names: Fitzpatrick, Elyse, 1950-
Title: Idols of the heart : learning to long for God alone / Elyse M.
   Fitzpatrick.
Description: Second edition. | Phillipsburg : P&R Pub., 2016. | "Revised and
   Updated."
Identifiers: LCCN 2015033580| ISBN 9781629952109 (pbk.) | ISBN 9781629952116
   (epub) | ISBN 9781629952123 (mobi)
Subjects: LCSH: Women--Religious life. | Idolatry.
Classification: LCC BV4527 .F586 2016 | DDC 248.8/43—dc23
LC record available at http://lccn.loc.gov/2015033580

To Phil for his steadfast love and patience:
It's because you laid down your life day after day
that I was able to do this.

Contents

Illustrations

A Note for the Second Edition

Over the years since I wrote the original manuscript for this book, I've become more and more aware of God's great love for me in Christ. I've grown to see how, because of His compassion and mercy, He loves me whether I'm fighting my idols diligently or just sort of meandering my way through the day. He knows my weakness: the weakness of my love, the weakness of my mind, the weakness of my determination to love Him more than all else. And yet He loves me because of the work His Son has done for me in justifying me and calling me beautiful . . . even though I fall so far short of His perfect standard, embodied in His law as expressed in the Ten Commandments.

So although I still desire to develop wholehearted worship, to "long for God Alone," and to help you do the same, my perspective on how to get there and what that actually means has changed. It has changed from looking primarily at myself to looking chiefly at Jesus' work for me in the gospel. That shift in focus also transforms the way I will talk about idolatry in this book and how I think our hearts are ultimately transformed. So in this book you'll hear more talk about love and more talk about God's love for sinners, all to and for the glory of the Son. It's not that I no longer care about obedience to the first commandment, it's just that I'm walking a different path toward that goal and have a different motivation propelling me onward.

Acknowledgments

Nothing worthwhile can ever be accomplished without the help and support of many people. If the Lord graciously uses this book to help anyone, it's because He's gifted me with godly family and friends who know what it means to fervently love Him. I know that I've never had a truly original thought, so I'm thankful to George Scipione for my training (and now for my son's wife); to Dave Powlison, who selflessly took ten minutes at a conference in the early 1990s and reconfigured my thinking about idolatry; to Pastor Dave Eby at North City Presbyterian Church (his sermon notes are all over this book); to my brothers and sisters in Christ who have prayed for me, encouraged me, and asked me, "How's the book coming? How can I pray for you?" I'm thankful for the ministry of John and Sandra Cully, Linda Quails, and John Hickernell at Evangelical Bible Bookstore, who kept me stocked with Puritan books and made great suggestions. Special thanks need to go to Anita Manata, Donna Turner, and Barbara Duguid, dear friends who were my sounding boards and helped me immensely in my thinking; to my mother for her kind suggestions and grammatical editing; and to Barbara Lerch at P&R, who believed that it was time for a Reformed woman to be heard on this topic.

It's impossible for me to properly acknowledge everyone who has loved and supported me throughout the many years since this book came out in 2001. I've been blessed by many friends who are listed above, including my friends at P&R Publishing, especially Ian Thompson, who saw the value of updating this book and offering it again to my audience.

I'm especially thankful for my dear family: Phil, James and Michelle, Jessica and Cody, Joel and Ruth, and all their beautiful little kidlets: Wesley, Hayden, Eowyn, Allie, Gabe, and Colin. I'm so blessed.

Introduction

Observing the World's Gods

During the spring of 1998 my husband and I and our cousins had the privilege of touring East Asia, spending about twelve days in China, South Korea, and Japan. Because we were with tour groups, we visited a number of Buddhist temples. We saw the oldest Buddha, the largest Buddha, the most venerated Buddha. We saw a Buddha that had been stolen during a battle and a Buddha that had been damaged by fire and rebuilt. We were asked to donate to a fund set up so that a certain Buddha could be refurbished in gold. We saw the Buddha that belonged to the emperor and the Buddha that belonged to the common people. We watched as worshipers lit candles and burned incense, offered prayers and set bowls of food and flowers before their gods. By the time the tour was over, my husband and I had seen enough idols to last us a lifetime. Or had we?

We were glad to return to the United States, a country with a Christian foundation. Unlike the Asian countries we visited, the United States doesn't have idols on every corner and days set aside to burn incense or light lanterns to our gods. We don't have large temples where we offer bowls of rice . . . or in our parlance, French fries. In fact, one survey found that 76 percent of Americans polled "consider themselves completely true to the First Commandment,"[1]

---

1. George Barna, *The Barna Report 1992–93, an Annual Survey of Lifestyles, Values, and Religious Views* (Carol Stream, IL: Christianity Today, Inc., 1995), 113, quoted in R. Kent Hughes, *Disciplines of Grace* (Wheaton, IL: Crossway, 1993), 29.

"You shall have no other gods before Me" (Ex. 20:3). So, when it comes to the first commandment, we're doing a pretty good job, right?

I imagine that if you're like me, you tend to think about idols in the terms that I've just described. Idols are something outside us; they're something foreign, something you take pictures of in far-off temples, something you wonder at.

The Gods in Our Heart

For me one of the most daunting commands in all of Scripture is in Matthew 22. Let me remind you how a scribe came to Jesus, seeking to find an avenue to accuse Him of heresy. "What is the most important of the commandments?" he asked. Jesus replied,

> "You shall love the Lord your God with all your heart, and with all your soul, and with all your mind." This is the great and foremost commandment. (Matt. 22:37–38)

Perhaps you're like me, and you've read that command so many times it's lost its impact. Go back now and reread it and think deeply with me for a moment. What is our Lord commanding here? Nothing less than undivided, perfect, and complete love and worship. Just as soon as I pause to reflect on that principal command, I begin to get uncomfortable. I have to ask myself,

- Do I love Him with everything that I am, or are there other loves in my heart that clamor for my attention?
- Do I worship additional gods, or is He always, and in every case, the supreme Ruler who receives my undivided passion and devotion?

When I think this way I begin to see that perhaps idolatry is something more than Buddhist temples, incense, and rice. Idolatry has to do with love—my love for Him, my love for others, my love of the world. When I look at idolatry in these ways, I understand that I'm not so different from those people I observed in temples so far away.

A Life Free from Idols

This book is written for those of you who desire to live a godly life and yet find yourself in a recurrently disappointing struggle against habitual sin and a lack of undivided love. This book is written for you who find yourself constantly tripping over the same bad habit, the same embarrassing weakness, the same sinful slavery that you hoped to be free of years ago. In this book you'll learn that idolatry—love gone wrong—lies at the heart of every besetting sin that we struggle with.

When you stop and think of it, the Bible is filled with stories about individuals and even nations falling into idolatry. In fact, it's the most commonly discussed sin in all of Scripture. First Corinthians 10:11 says that the Old Testament stories are an example for us, that "they were written for our instruction."

One of the first stories about idolatry is that of Rachel, Jacob's wife. Because Rachel's problem with idolatry is so prominent in her narrative, we'll be looking into her life frequently in this book—discovering how her failures might instruct us. We'll also see how the stories of others in Scripture, both men and women, enlighten and inform us about our false gods today. You will notice that some of the following chapters begin with vignettes. These stories are not directly from Scripture, but are my interpretation of what might have happened. They are not to be taken as strictly biblical, and are only illustrative.

Since the Bible is God's Word to His children, children whom He knows thoroughly, there must be a reason why He's inserted so much teaching on this subject . . . even though it may seem to us that idolatry isn't that big of a concern. (Remember that 76 percent of all Americans polled thought they were guiltless in this area!) As you read further, you'll discover that idolatry is just as big of a problem for us today as it was for the Israelites of old. In fact, perhaps it's even bigger—because we've conveniently categorized idolatry as something that exists outside us (little stone statues) rather than something that lives within our hearts. Even though idolatry is commonly spoken of and even confessed in some circles, I wonder whether we've actually begun to scratch the surface of the pervasiveness of this sin.

In the chapters to come you'll learn the ways in which the focus of your love and the focus of your worship are similar. *Whom do you love? And whom do you worship?* are crucial questions that are linked together. You'll learn to identify the false gods that live in your heart: in your thoughts and your affections. And then you'll learn about God's method of freeing you from your idols, your "love-gone-wrong," by His sanctifying power.

I want you to know that my struggle with sin and idolatry is the same as yours—the same as Rachel's. Like her, we all struggle with putting our hope and trust in something, someone, anything other than the true God. We find ourselves weak, afraid, fretting or angry, bitter and complaining. In the midst of this struggle, I believe that God's voice is calling us: clearly, lovingly bringing illumination and liberation, reminding us of His incomparable love for us and His gracious welcome of idolaters.

Although our war with sin will continue until heaven, God has covenanted Himself to faithfully enable us to grow in holiness. He invites us to join in this battle with Him, and He's given us weapons to use in this struggle. One of the weapons He's given us is knowledge. Not knowledge that consists in mere lifeless facts, but rather a dynamic awareness of the realities of our personal struggle with wayward loves and God's faithfulness to accomplish our deliverance both for this life and all eternity.

Microwaveable Holiness

I love the convenience of the microwave, don't you? Just pop the casserole in and, presto, instant dinner. Life is better in our house since the invention of the microwave. I can defrost dinner ten minutes before I need to make it . . . and with my scatteredness, that's a real blessing! I enjoy all of our modern conveniences, don't you? But in the middle of this instant, *Give it to me quickly! It better be convenient!* culture, we tend to think that God should work in our lives in the same way. *Just zap me and make me holy—and quickly, Lord, if You don't mind.*

God's work in us is most of the time maddeningly slow. Although it's true that all Christians know some change (even if it's minuscule), God's work—our sanctification—is a process. This process involves learning (what I hope you'll do here), growing, falling, changing, becoming convinced again of the truth, failing again, and developing wholeness over our lifetimes. With that in mind, don't expect that this book will transform you instantly or cure your heart of its wayward loves. Only God through His Holy Spirit can transform your desires, and He has a different timetable than we do. He knows what struggles we need to continue to face, and He knows how, under the influence of His Spirit, even our failures in those struggles will make us love Him and His good news more.

Hope in Christ Alone

As we begin this journey together, let me remind you of a truth that I'm sure you already know. *God changes hearts.* Our loving heavenly Father has committed Himself to our transformation, first from darkness to light, and second from the loves of our former life to love under the banner of His "It is finished." He's given us everything we need for growth in life and godliness that He has ordained. He's given us every tool we need to fight against our idols and to grow in grace; not only that, He's committed all the resources of heaven to His goal:

- He's given us Jesus Christ, who perfectly loved and worshipped His Father. His perfect life of obedience (both outward and inward) is now our record: even though we still struggle with love gone wrong, He never did, and our Father sees only His perfect record when He looks at us. We are counted completely faithful, completely loving, and completely holy *already*.
- Not only did He live a perfect life for us, He also paid for all our errant loves, all our idolatries, in His excruciating death on Calvary where His Father accounted Him as the worst idolater of all time. All the idolatry you have or will ever give into has already been atoned for by His shameful death on the cross. In Christ, the Father has no wrath left for you. Will the Father turn His back on you for your idolatry? No, never. Because He already deserted His Son in your place.
- Because He has completely fulfilled the Law, we are now free from sin's bondage. We're no longer rebels responding to the Law's decrees as slaves; instead we view the Law as a guide to help us know how to love, rather than as a way to earn His approval or avoid punishment. The Law shows us how to respond in gratitude for the truth that it no longer has the power to condemn us because Jesus has fulfilled it all.

- We can also rejoice because we know that Jesus Christ, our Advocate, is praying for us, interceding for us, even though we are sorely tempted and tried. Because of His prayer, we can know that our faith will never fail. We can rest confidently in Him.
- He's endowed us with His Holy Spirit, who indwells us and guides us into truth. The Holy Spirit's work is to remind us of all the gifts we've been given in Christ. He pours out His grace upon us, assures us that we are His beloved (though often struggling) children. It's this grace that enables us to desire to do His will and respond in love to His love.
- He's provided us with the Word of Truth: truth that illumines our hearts to all the wisdom that we need to change in a way that pleases Him. He's done this for the ultimate goal of changing us—and all for His glory!

In 1998 I took a twelve-day tour visiting the idols of East Asia. You too have begun a journey—but it will probably take longer than twelve days . . . so settle in for the journey and rejoice in the knowledge that God will use His Word and His Spirit to reveal your idols, your love-gone-wrong, and to develop wholehearted love and devotion in you—all for His glory and praise!

1

Rachel's Gods and You

Little children, guard yourselves
from idols. (1 John 5:21)

"Go get your things.[1] You and Leah get the children and get ready to go," her husband commanded. "We're leaving tonight."

"Tonight? Right now? But I'm not ready!"

Rachel loved her husband, but she also enjoyed the blessing of living near her parents. Even though she enjoyed the closeness of the families, things weren't always peaceful between them. It seemed as though there was continual strife between her husband and her father. And now, the event she had dreaded was transpiring.

"Don't forget your cloak," she told Joseph. "Stop bickering with the other children, and gather up your things."

In the same ways that you and I would, Rachel gathered up all the household items that were important to her. Then, in the midst of her frenzy, reality set in and a chill ran through her heart. *I'm really leaving my home . . . everything I've ever known. How can I know that I'll be cared for? How can I know that I'll be safe? How can I get along without my father's protection . . . without his gods?*

---

1. If you aren't already familiar with the story of Jacob, Rachel, Leah, and Laban, take time to read it beginning in Genesis 29.

And so, after her father had left home to go work in the field, she went into his house and stole his household idols from him. Although she didn't realize it at the time, her actions would soon jeopardize her family and bring about another act of deception. Instead of bringing security, these idols would place her family at risk. Instead of blessing her, they would be a curse.

A Familiar Story

We've all read the story of Rachel's theft in Genesis 31. Although this is the first time idols are mentioned in the Bible, it would be easy to pass over it and miss the enormity of the act and its consequences: Rachel stole from her father. She took his gods. She deceived her husband and endangered her family. Later, when Laban, her father, questioned her about the disappearance of his idols, she deceived him again.

I've often wondered why she thought she had to have those idols. What did they mean to her? Why was she willing to do what she did? Why were they so powerful in her life?

In order to answer these questions, let's look at Rachel's life. We know the Bible says that "Rachel was beautiful of form and face" (Gen. 29:17). In today's vernacular, Rachel was a real knockout. Rachel undoubtedly knew that when it came to feminine charms, she had her sister Leah beat hands down. She must have relished the favor that was hers. Rachel had learned that she could trust in her own beauty; her beauty was, in fact, her justification. It was what she rested in, what she believed made her "okay" in the eyes of others and in her own eyes. It was the source of her power over others, her protection from disappointment. She was so beautiful that when Jacob first laid eyes on her, he knew she was the one for him. In their first meeting she captured his heart, and he served her father fourteen years for her.[2] In fact, he loved her so much that the years he spent working to secure her for himself "seemed to him but a few days" (Gen. 29:20). That's real devotion! With a beginning like this, you would think that the rest of Rachel's life would have been a bed of roses. She was beautiful, and she had her husband's love . . . what else could she possibly want?

"Give Me Children!"

As time went by the answer to that question became evident. What more could she possibly want? Children! She had to sit idly by while her elder (and ugly) sister Leah gave birth to six sons . . . and still Rachel was barren. Every time one of those boys cried, or whenever Jacob played with one of them, Rachel's jealousy must have grown. She must have been filled with doubt, anger, and self-pity as she felt her favored position was eroding. The god she had worshipped, her beauty, was powerless to save her, and she was desperate to obtain the approval and position she thought was her birthright. Her beautiful eyes could do nothing to fill her empty uterus.

"Give me children, or else I die!" she finally cried despairingly. "Am I in the place of God?" Jacob angrily retorted (Gen. 30:1–2). Rachel's desire for children was so strong that it had twisted her thinking. She began to believe that it was Jacob rather than God who was controlling her fertility, her position, and her life. She felt naked and worthless; her barrenness was an ugliness she couldn't stand to look at.

In time, God graciously gave Rachel a son. Don't miss the kindness of God's act of grace here. God wasn't responding to her pure heart or holy desires. He blessed her despite her unbelief.

---

2. In a perfect example of sowing and reaping, Jacob, the deceiver of his father, was deceived by his father-in-law.

Then, although she was temporarily filled with joy at his birth, she still wasn't content. Her heart was revealed by her naming of him, "May the LORD give me another son" (Gen. 30:24). Rachel wasn't satisfied with the blessing that God had given her in Joseph. She wanted more. And that, dear friends, is always and ever the outcome of idolatry: it always ends in dissatisfaction.

Rachel did eventually conceive again, and as she was dying in childbirth, she named this son Benoni, which means "son of my sorrow." What she had worshiped and thought would bring her blessing ended up causing her death. What she thought would bring her joy brought her sorrow instead. It is ironic, isn't it, that the woman who cried, "Give me children or I'll die!" died in childbirth? Her life demonstrates the truth that there is no life in idolatry. All it brings is death.

You see, even before Rachel stole her father's idols she was an idolater. Her desire to have children like her sister Leah was the most important thing in her life. It was something she believed that she had to have, and so it was her god. Rachel believed in justification by mothering; she thought she had to earn her "okay-ness" before God, others, and herself. She had never known what it was to be unable to approve of herself. And now she was drowning in shame and sorrows.

Rachel's Gods

It's not hard to imagine that Rachel had always been the center of attention, that life had always gone her way. She probably wasn't used to Leah having a position of favor over her. Because of her infertility and everything it represented to her, Rachel had come face to face with an insurmountable problem—something she may have never experienced before. She feared that she had to take steps to protect her position. She believed her father's gods would somehow bless her, so she took them. Perhaps she believed that there might be a God who ruled over the earth, but He was too far away and too unmanageable for her comfort. She couldn't trust Him to order life as she desired. She needed a tamer, more docile god—one she could control. She wanted a god that would give her what she needed. She wanted a god she could steal, one she could hide![3] She wanted a god she could keep in her purse.

My Household Idols

As I've thought about Rachel's story, I've wondered whether I have any domestic deities—household gods that I'm looking to for my happiness, security, and self-justification. What do I long for so much that my heart clamors, "Give me *this*, or else I'll die!" What must I have for life to be meaningful or happy? What enables me to lie down at night and know that, at my core, I'm really okay? If I answer that question with anything other than God Himself, then that's what functions as a god for me.

Even though we don't bow down to stone statues or make bowls of food to set before our gods, we worship idols in other ways. John Calvin commented on this when he wrote, "When [Moses] relates that Rachel stole her father's idols, he is speaking of a vice that was common. From this we may gather that man's nature . . . is a perpetual *factory of idols*."[4]

Idols aren't just stone statues. No, idols are the loves, thoughts, desires, longings, and expectations that we worship in the place of the true God. They are the things that we invest our identity in;

3. "Now Rachel had taken the household idols and put them in the camel's saddle, and she sat on them. And Laban felt through all the tent but did not find them. She said to her father, 'Let not my lord be angry that I cannot rise before you, for the manner of women is upon me.' So he searched but did not find the household idols" (Gen. 31:34–35).

4. John Calvin, *Institutes of the Christian Religion*, ed. John T. McNeill, 2 vols., Library of Christian Classics (Philadelphia: Westminster, 1960), 1:108. Emphasis added.

they are what we trust. Idols cause us to disregard our heavenly Father in search of what we think we need. Our idols are our loves-gone-wrong: all those things we love more than we love Him, the things we trust for our righteousness or "okay-ness."

Covenantal Gods

In some ways, the relationship that we have with these false gods is similar to the relationship that we have with the true God. We look to these gods to bless us. We make covenants with them; we endow them with the power to bless us if we work hard enough for them. For instance, Rachel would say, "If I have children like my sister Leah, I'll be happy!" Or we might say, "If I have a godly spouse" or "If my children excel in school, I'll be happy." Of course having godly relationships is a blessing and a source of happiness, and there is nothing sinful in desiring them; but if they are the source of our joy, if they take top priority in our lives, then they are our gods.

Jesus said, "Seek first [God's] kingdom and His righteousness" (Matt. 6:33). If building His kingdom (and not our own) is the top priority in our lives, we will rest in the knowledge that everything we ultimately need will be ours because of His great love, and then the demands that these idols make on us will diminish. For instance the idol of obedient children that drives us to pick at them or criticize them will lose its impetus if we're not trying to build the kingdom of our family. Further, if we seek the righteousness that comes from God alone (Rom. 10:3–4) rather than our own, we won't pressure our family to perform so that we can feel good about ourselves or try to justify ourselves with the reputation of "good parent."

Let's look more closely at how the worship of false gods plays out in our lives.

"Give Me a Godly Husband, or I'll Die!"

Jenny believed that the only way for her to be happy was to have a godly husband. She was married to a Christian man who attended church with her, but she wanted a husband who would pray regularly with her and who would have devotions with the family. I agreed with her that it would have been a blessing for him to be a more godly leader. I also tried to encourage him to find other men who might help him grow.

As I got to know Jenny, though, I saw that her desire for a godly husband functioned like a god in her life. The thought "I must have a godly husband or I'll die" ruled her. Sometimes she thought that if she was extra nice and made him the dinner that he liked, he would be obligated to fulfill her desires. On other days she would give up in frustration and anger, withholding herself from him and pouting. Like Rachel, she was convinced that she could not find happiness unless her expectations were met. Her self-approval and identity were located in his growth as a leader. And so, it wasn't terribly surprising that a day came when she told me that she was going to leave him. She left him and the church, and the last that I heard she was no longer following Christ. Like Rachel, her desire ended up destroying her.

Venerated Blessings

An integral part of false worship is earning merit so that we can get false gods to give us what we want. In essence, we make covenants with them, expecting them to bless us if we act in certain ways.

For instance, if good health is a god to you, you might think: "If I exercise every day and eat properly, I'll never get ill." If having meaningful employment is a god to you, you might think:

"If I'm always the first at my desk and always doing more than is required of me, then my employer will be obligated to notice me and protect my job." Please don't misunderstand. I'm not saying that it is wrong to exercise properly or work diligently; not only are we to value the good gift God has given us in our body, but we are also commanded to shun murder, including murder that is self-inflicted through poor use of food or exercise. If motivated by love of God and others, each of these things can be good. But these actions become sinful when we do them primarily out of sinful fear, to earn merit, or to manipulate outcomes rather than freely out of a heart of gratitude for God. The only holy reason for doing any good is the love of the Lord and our neighbor. If a good resume or lean body is the way you seek to justify yourself, you will find that no matter how hard you try, you'll never be able to satisfy the demands of gym or employer. There is no rest in idolatry.

I can imagine that you might be wondering, "Okay, Elyse, how can I tell if I'm worshiping the blessings that I desire or God?" Although we're going to look at that question in more depth in following chapters, let me summarize in this way: if you're willing to sin to obtain your goal or if you sin when you don't get what you want, then your desire has taken God's place and you are functioning as an idolater.

Remember how Rachel sinned? She was sinfully angry with her husband; she stole her father's gods and deceived her family. Later, she wasn't content with the birth of Joseph and wanted more children. It wasn't idolatrous for Rachel to desire children. No, she was idolatrous because her desire for children was the foremost desire in her heart. "Give me children, or else I die!" is the cry of an idolater.

Think with me about the command Jesus said was most important. He said that the primary love in your heart has to be centered on God. Anything less than that is idolatry. If you work very hard at your job and are still passed over for the promotion, your response will reveal whether you're serving God or worshiping an idol. Is God and your love for Him more important than your job? Or if you make a nice dinner for your husband and he ignores you, watches television, goes to bed, and you get angry and cry or pout or look for ways to punish him, you can know that your love for God isn't the predominant love in your life.

Certain Curses

It's in the covenantal nature of worship to believe that your god can bless or curse you. Rachel believed that barrenness was a curse that was intolerable. We know that because she was willing to give up anything to avoid it. That's always how idols function in our hearts. We sell ourselves to them, and we believe that the loss of them will be an unbearable affliction—a curse. That's why they are so powerful in our lives.

There is a curse involved in idolatry, but it isn't because we don't get what we want. The curse is that we're trusting in something other than God to satisfy us. Consider Jeremiah 17:5–6:

> Thus says the Lord,
> "Cursed is the man who trusts in mankind
> And makes flesh his strength,
> And whose heart turns away from the Lord.
> "For he will be like a bush in the desert
> And will not see when prosperity comes,
> But will live in stony wastes in the wilderness,
> A land of salt without inhabitant."

What do you notice about the man who trusts in something other than God? He's never satisfied. He's like a thirsty bush in the desert, a bramble in the wilderness. What could be more dissatisfying?

I remember taking a Jeep tour into the Sonoran Desert. Although it was springtime and it had rained recently, that desert was desolate. Our guide kept telling us to be careful because there were no friendly plants or animals there. In fact, everything that grew there was dangerous to get near. There were thorns on one cactus that had microscopic reverse barbs—if you even brushed by them, they would grab you. Another cactus had three-inch thorns so sharp and strong that you could push them through four folds of denim with ease. This was a wilderness, a land without inhabitant. Although I enjoyed our little trip, I must admit that I was glad to get back into that Jeep and head for civilization. It wasn't anyplace I'd like to live permanently, that's certain. The Bible teaches that when I center my trust and love on myself, my desires, my ability to save myself, or anything other than God, then that's exactly where I live . . . in the desert.

It would be a curse to be forced to live in a wilderness, wouldn't it? The person who trusts in or loves anything more than God is cursed because he's so focused on what he wants that he doesn't even notice when good things happen. All he can see is what is missing from his life. That's because his heart has turned away from loving the Lord, and he loves something else more. He loves his own self-righteousness, his self-sufficiency and his self-approval. And that's why Rachel could be beautiful, have the undivided love of her husband, and give birth to a healthy baby boy and still cry, "I want more." Rachel lived in a desert in more than one way. She lived in a desert created by her desires. Her life was miserable, sad, futile, and hopeless because she had discovered that she wasn't the perfect woman. The worship of idols is the reason we're discontented, and it's why we disobey God. And Calvin says that our hearts manufacture them.

Bury Your Idols

What did Rachel eventually do with her idols? You'll be glad that they probably ended up buried under a tree. Jacob charged his family to return to God. "Put away the foreign gods which are among you," he told his family. "So they gave to Jacob all the foreign gods which they had . . . and Jacob hid them under the oak which was near Shechem" (Gen. 35:2, 4). We can hope that Rachel surrendered her false gods at her husband's command. Even though she died soon after, there's no reason to believe that she held on to them despite her husband's command. Perhaps God delivered Rachel from her belief that she needed something other than Him—perhaps He turned her heart to trust only in Him.

You too can rest today knowing that as you, by His grace, respond to your heavenly Husband's command to surrender your idols, He'll bury them under another tree. By His power He can bury all our false gods under the most awesome and glorious tree ever . . . the one on Golgotha's mount. You can trust Him with all your fears, all your desires, all your sin, because He is the One who said, "It is finished."

Is Rachel's story relevant to you and me? Yes, it is—because idolatry didn't end with her. This problem continues on into the church today. We must remember John's final words, "Little children, guard yourselves from idols" (1 John 5:21). His warning to "beware of" or "watch against" false worship is lost on us if we don't comprehend how our hearts manufacture idols.

God calls us to bury our false gods at the cross. It's in union with Jesus Christ, the one who hung on Golgotha's tree, that we have the desire and power to conquer all our idolatry and bury our gods in the blood-soaked ground beneath His cross.

Only God the Heart Knower is also the Heart Changer. The God who knows and loves us completely, more than we can comprehend, also knows all our desires and the place that they occupy in our love. It is He who is the Heart Changer. The writer of Hebrews said,

> And there is no creature hidden from His sight, but all things are open and laid bare to the eyes of Him with whom we have to do. . . . For we do not have a high priest who cannot sympathize with our weaknesses, but One who has been tempted in all things as we are, yet without sin. Therefore let us draw near with confidence to the throne of grace, so that we may receive mercy and find grace to help in time of need. (Heb. 4:13, 15–16)

Every desire in our heart, whether idolatrous in essence or idolatrous because of our inordinate love for it, is known to our Father. Everything is "open and laid bare" before Him, and He knows us thoroughly. He knows every time that we put something before Him, that we love something more than we love Him. If that were the end of the story, we would despair, wouldn't we? Praise God that the passage goes on to say that our dear Savior, our High Priest, sympathizes with our weaknesses. He understands our diluted worship and implores us to draw near to Him, so that we might "receive mercy and find grace to help in time of need." We desperately need His mercy and help in our conflict with idolatry . . . and He's promised to give it. So focus all your hope and trust on Him. I know that He'll prove Himself a faithful High Priest, granting you the help you need to develop a heart and life wholly focused on loving and worshiping Him.

When you find yourself worried, angry, or fearful, like Rachel, you can rest knowing that you don't need to grab an idol off a shelf or find some other way to take care of yourself. God's mercy and grace is available to you every moment—and His promised help is as certain as His character. You can step toward Him . . . He knows you and what you worship . . . and He's more than able to sustain you in your time of need. So go ahead and draw near to Him with confidence. You'll find that He's full of sympathy and more than able to support and change you. After all, He's already counted you righteous in Christ. What more do you need?

FOR FURTHER THOUGHT

1. Think about the story of Rachel and Leah. If you aren't familiar with it, you can read it beginning in Genesis 29. Do you identify more with Rachel or Leah? How does God's dealings with both of them comfort or encourage you?

2. Think about the areas of your life in which you struggle with sin. Can you see any connection between your habitual sin and any possible idolatry? If so, write it down. If not, don't be dismayed; the Lord will help you see if there are any idols in your heart.

3. Is there anything in your life that you think you must have?

4. How would you complete this sentence: "Give me _____ or I'll die!" Are you looking to some earthly Jacob to provide ultimate satisfaction for you? What words do you use to comfort yourself when you're faced with failure or disappointment?

5. Write out a prayer of commitment stating your desire to understand how your heart might manufacture idols.

2

Undivided Adoration

"Do you love Me more than these?"
(John 21:15)

It seems as though all I ever do is work. I don't suppose that it even dawns on my sister that I'd like to sit and listen to the Teacher's words, too. Why doesn't she see that I need help? Sometimes she's so selfish! I've got so many things to do to prepare for the dinner and our houseguests. I think that I'll go and tell her what I think.

As Martha left the kitchen and entered the living room, the sight of her sister sitting at the feet of Jesus aggravated her again. *Why doesn't Jesus make her help me? Why does He let her just sit there? Doesn't He care about me?*

"Lord," Martha demanded, "do You not care that my sister has left me to do all the serving alone? Then tell her to help me."

As the Lord lovingly looked into His distraught servant's face, He said, "Martha, Martha, you are worried and bothered about so many things; but only one thing is necessary, for Mary has chosen the good part, which shall not be taken away from her" (Luke 10:41–42).

I don't think I've ever met a Christian woman for whom Christ's words weren't piercingly convicting. It seems that serving in material ways is for some reason easier and more rewarding than sitting at the Lord's feet, listening to Him. Why is that? Does this inclination indicate a problem with our worship? our love? And what is that "good part" that Mary had chosen and Martha and many of us miss?

Loving God Too Much?

Have you ever met anyone who was too devoted to the Lord, who was too focused on loving Him? I haven't. In fact, I don't think it's possible. As Richard Baxter says, "Infinite goodness cannot possibly be loved too much."[1] I'm not talking about being devoted in some mystical way that precludes responsible living. I'm talking about the difficulty when we try to focus our daily lives, moment by moment, on loving, worshiping, and serving the Lord—on sitting at His feet.

I'm involved in Christian ministry on a pretty regular basis. But the questions that I am continually forced to ask myself are, *How much time am I spending at His feet? How much time do I spend on the one needful thing?* I'm not talking about prep time for my ministry opportunities—I'm talking about time sitting at His feet, worshiping Him. It's true . . . I'm just like Martha. I have strong competing loves in my heart. Yes, I love God, but I'm a little busy working for Him right now . . . so I'll spend time with Him later.

Even in my Christian ministry responsibilities, it's possible for me to worship gods of my own making . . . gods of my reputation, my plans for the day, my ideas. It's easy to get so frustrated and caught up in "serving" the Lord that I forget to love

---

1. Richard Baxter, *A Christian Directory* (Morgan, PA: Soli Deo Gloria Publications, 1996), 123.

and worship Him. It's during those times that I begin to think, like Martha, that God doesn't care about me. The truth about His love and sacrificial care is clouded by my plans and desires. And it's also true that much of the work we do "for" the Lord is actually a way for us to try to save ourselves, to merit blessings, or to justify our existence.

Martha's problem isn't unique. That's why we hear the Lord's words to Martha echoed in His teachings to others. "Do not work for the food which perishes, but for the food which endures to eternal life, which the Son of Man will give to you" (John 6:27). "Be on guard, so that your hearts will not be weighted down with . . . the worries of life" (Luke 21:34). Why is it so easy for us to get weighted down and entrapped? It's because, as John Calvin said, our hearts manufacture other gods, gods that we presume will save us and provide for us.

Does it ever seem to you that the Bible is filled with astounding understatements? Exodus 20:3 says, "You shall have no other gods before Me." In this simple statement the Lord God, Creator of the heavens and earth, directs our entire focus and destiny. Our response to these eight short words, so seemingly inconsequential, influences every facet of our lives, now and eternally. Is the one needful thing that Mary found and Martha missed encapsulated in this terse command? Did Martha have another god installed before Jehovah?

The Puritans' Insights

As we seek understanding of the undivided devotion God demands in the first commandment, the Westminster Larger Catechism will help us.

The catechism poses the question, "What are the duties required in the first commandment?" The answer that the writers of the catechism give is so helpful in elaborating the full intent of the commandment that I'll quote it in its entirety (although it's a little lengthy):

> The duties required in the first commandment are, the knowing and acknowledging of God to be the only true God, and our God; and to worship and glorify him accordingly, by thinking, meditating, remembering, highly esteeming, honoring, adoring, choosing, loving, desiring, fearing of him; believing him; trusting, hoping, delighting, rejoicing in him; being zealous for him; calling upon him, giving all praise and thanks, and yielding all obedience and submission to him with the whole man; being careful in all things to please him, and sorrowful when in anything he is offended; and walking humbly with him.[2]

Why not go back and reread their answer again? Every one of those verbs is significant and rich with meaning, isn't it? As I read over them, I can plainly see how I fail to know, acknowledge, worship, and glorify God as my only true God. Think with me as I go partially through the list:

- *Thinking about God.* Do I think of God continually or only infrequently, such as when I want or need something?
- *Meditating on God.* Do I meditate on His character— His holiness, His goodness, His love?
- *Remembering God.* Do I remember Him in everything I do and say, or do I rarely think of Him?
- *Trusting God.* Am I really trusting in Him, or do I trust in other things like my resume or work?

---

2. The Larger Catechism, Q. 104 (Carlisle, PA: Banner of Truth Trust, 1998).

Can you appreciate the practical insight of the Puritans? Although the first commandment might be mistaken by some people as ambiguous, the Puritans have nailed it down in practical, day-to-day terms, haven't they? Let's take time now to more thoroughly study two of their terms: *honoring* and *trusting*.

A Priest Who Didn't Honor God

Before the time of Israel's kings, a priest named Eli acted as God's ruler. Eli had a significant problem: he didn't honor God. Even though He served Jehovah and had the highest position of authority in the temple, he thought more of pleasing his two rebellious sons than of pleasing God. That was obvious because when his sons acted in ungodly ways, he didn't discipline them.[3] God challenged Eli about his sin: "Why do you . . . honor your sons above Me?" (1 Sam. 2:29). Because Eli honored his sons above God, it was inevitable that his priesthood would end.

Even though Eli served the Lord, pleasing his sons was more important than honoring God. Although he probably never said it, his actions spoke louder than any words. Eli thought more of peace in his household than peace with God, so he neglected his duty and brought disgrace on the Lord. The pleasure of having a peaceful relationship with his sons functioned as his god. He served this cherished ideal and ignored God's commands to discipline his children. Eli, though he was a priest, was an idolater. Although he didn't bow down to stone images, he bowed to his children's demands—even when they conflicted with God's.

3. "Now the sons of Eli were worthless men; they did not know the LORD. . . . Thus the sin of the young men was very great before the LORD, for the men despised the offering of the LORD" (1 Sam. 2:12, 17). See also 1 Sam. 2:22–25, 29; "For I have told him that I am about to judge his house forever for the iniquity which he knew, because his sons brought a curse on themselves and he did not rebuke them" (1 Sam. 3:13).

As those who worship God, our concern for God's honor should be so strong that the natural love that we have for others should seem like hate in comparison. As Jesus said, "If anyone comes to Me, and does not hate his own father and mother and wife and children and brothers and sisters, yes, and even his own life, he cannot be My disciple" (Luke 14:26).

As I look back over my life as a mom, I can see numbers of ways that I bowed to my children's demands rather than honoring God. I can see how I acquiesced to their desires and gave them what they wanted because I wanted to pamper them or make them happy. Sometimes I wanted to be their friend so much that I didn't care about my friendship with God. Other times I even fought against my husband's leadership because I didn't want their displeasure. In my heart, I'm like Eli. There were times that I made an idol of my children's good opinion . . . and like Martha I'm missing that one necessary thing: the worship of God.

Honoring God means that the Lord's pleasure and glory come first. It means giving respect and deference to Him and esteeming Him above the opinions of those we love. It means that we are willing to suffer disrespect and even persecution in order to respect Him. We can detect the worship of false gods in our hearts when we honor anything above God.

A Father Who Trusted God

Another facet of the worship of God is trust. Trusting God means having confidence in Him and obeying His commands, no matter what the cost. It means I believe that all I need to be loved and cared for eternally has already been given to me in Christ.

Trust is one of those bedrock issues that I have to continuously work on. Even though I trust Christ for my eternal salvation, I frequently encounter other areas of my life where I'm not trusting God. For instance, I find myself filled with worry if I think that there won't be enough money to pay the bills. Instead of trusting God's provision, I am tempted to nag my husband, become worried and angry, or give up in frustration and spend money in an effort to satisfy and calm my heart. In truth, these actions belie a lack of trust in God's ability to provide. They are the thoughts and actions of an idolater.

Abraham had waited for years for God's promised gift—a son whom God would use to bring His Deliverer into the world. After the birth of Isaac, God called Abraham to an obedience beyond imagination. "Take now your son, your only son," He commanded, "whom you love, Isaac, and go to the land of Moriah, and offer him there as a burnt offering" (Gen. 22:2). That Abraham submitted to God's command is an amazing example of how God sustains and empowers us to obey by His grace.

Abraham loved Isaac, and God knew it. In His command for this sacrifice, God pointed out that Isaac was the son whom Abraham loved. The Lord wanted Abraham to understand that He knew what He was asking. This wasn't the sacrifice of Ishmael.[4] This was Isaac, the favored son, the son of the promise through whom the Messiah was to come. It would have been easy for Abraham to assume that the coming of the Messiah rested solely on his ability to protect Isaac. After all, God's promise seemed to be contingent upon Isaac's growing to be a man. It would have been easy for Abraham to trust in himself and his ability as a father. Just like you and me, in the past Abraham had struggled with trying to work things out (even God's promises) in his own

---

4. See Gen. 16–17, 21, for the complete story of Abraham; Sarah's maid, Hagar; and their son, Ishmael.

way, trusting in himself.[5] He could have reasoned in his heart, *God wouldn't ask me to kill Isaac—no, my protection of Isaac is necessary for God to fulfill His plan for a Messiah . . . I have to do what I think is right.*

By God's grace, Abraham was enabled to trust in the Lord's power and plan. Hebrews 11 gives us insight into Abraham's thinking: "He considered that God is able to raise people even from the dead" (Heb. 11:19). Abraham had no assurances that God would provide a ram for the sacrifice—the only guarantee he had was God's promise, "in you all the families of the earth will be blessed" (Gen. 12:3). God could give him another son, He could raise Isaac from the dead, or He could fulfill His promise in another way. In any case, Abraham had learned to trust Him, so he got up early, taking wood, fire, and a knife, and set out to keep his appointment with the God he trusted. What kept him going during that three-day journey to Mount Moriah? Perhaps he simply trusted that God hadn't lied. He trusted in God's wisdom, power, and veracity. Perhaps he rehearsed God's promises:

I will make you a great nation. (Gen. 12:2)

I will make your descendants as the dust of the earth. (Gen. 13:16)

Count the stars. . . . So shall your descendants be. (Gen. 15:5)

---

5. Although Abraham came through this test with flying colors, it wasn't always that way in his life. In Gen. 12:13 and 20:2, he twice endangered Sarah, who was to be the mother of the promised son, by telling the kings of the land she was merely his sister. It was a sign of God's providential grace that He kept her from sexual relations with any of the king's court, thereby protecting the godly line. The actions belie the fact that Abraham trusted in his ability and schemes to protect himself. In Gen. 16 he gives in to Sarah's schemes and has sexual relations with Hagar, producing a son by his own power, again questioning God's ability to fulfill His word.

I am God Almighty. . . . And I will multiply you exceedingly. (Gen. 17:1–2)

I will make you exceedingly fruitful, and I will make nations of you, and kings will come forth from you. (Gen. 17:6)

By God's grace and power, Abraham believed His promises and willingly obeyed.

Consider the differences between Abraham's and Eli's relationships with God. Abraham loved his son, but he loved God more. He worshiped God and was willing to do so even if it cost him the person dearest to his heart. Yes, Abraham loved his son, but his love seemed like hatred in comparison with the love that he had for His God. Eli would have said that he loved both God and his sons. But his actions proved that, when push came to shove, his sons ruled in his heart.

Trusting the God You Worship

In the face of adversity, when it seems as though everything you've worked for is about to go up in smoke—when the kids are ill, or the bottom falls out of your business, or the church is in turmoil—the bottom-line questions have to be the following: Do you trust God? Do you believe that He's wise, good, and powerful enough to perform all His will and bring you and your family safely to Him? Can you hear Him saying to you, "I am God Almighty"?

I would like to say that I always trust God in that way, but I don't. Instead, I frequently find myself hedging my bets and questioning God's goodness and truthfulness. I do believe that God is good and that I can trust His word, but that belief is always in competition with other beliefs and fears in my heart:

- You can trust God for salvation and those religious things, but when it comes to your marriage, you need to follow your way.
- You don't need to try to push yourself to live a life of grateful obedience in response to God's welcome and love. Your disobedience isn't idolatry; your circumstances are special.

It is in these not-so-subtle ways that I find I fail in obedience to the first commandment and set up other gods—gods of my reason, gods of self-exaltation, self-salvation and self-love—instead of developing wholehearted trust and devotion. Let me give you one more example that might help you to see how easy it is to be confused about the focus of our love.

"Do You Love Me More Than These?"

Prior to his denial of Christ on the night of His crucifixion, Peter thought that he possessed an undivided adoration for his Lord. He would have fit in with the 76 percent of Americans who believe they keep the first commandment. He wrongly assumed that his love for the Lord was stronger than any other love. "Even if I have to die with You," he insisted, "I will not deny You!" (Mark 14:31). "Truly I say to you," Jesus answered, "that this very night . . . you yourself will deny Me three times" (Mark 14:30).

What a shock those words must have been to self-assured, proud Peter! But what was probably even more shocking, what shook him to the foundations of his soul, was the look of love and understanding Jesus gave him after he had denied Him (Luke 22:61). As Peter's gaze connected with the Lord's, he understood the inconsistencies of his heart, the frailty of his love, and the true focus of his love. He had other gods. Once Peter had thought he was strong enough to be his own savior. "He went out and wept bitterly" (Luke 22:62).

Peter had twice seen the Lord after His resurrection,[6] but he was still struggling with his sin and the competing loves in his heart. Mercifully Jesus helped him to understand his weakness. On the beach, as Jesus made breakfast for His disciples, He lovingly confronted Peter. Three times he asked him, "Simon, son of John, do you love Me more than these?" (John 21:15). In the Greek, Jesus asked Peter, "Do you love me with an all-consuming devotion that rules out all other loves?" Twice Peter skirted the issue and declared that he had strong affection for the Lord. The third time Jesus changed the question and asked him, "Do you have a strong affection for me?" Peter in distress and sorrow was forced to admit, "Lord, You know all things; You know that I love You" (John 21:17). It was as if Peter was finally saying, "Lord, you know my heart. You know the loves that contend for my attention there. I do love You, but you know how I have failed to love You by loving other things, especially people and their opinion of me. Do I love you more than these? Is my love stronger than theirs? Lord, only you know." In essence the Lord's answer to him was, "Yes, Peter, I do know. And now, so do you. Now serve Me by caring for people, but in doing so remember whom you are serving. Remember whom you are to worship. Remember that I'm the only One strong enough to save. And remember that you aren't any better than those you serve."

The Lord knew that Peter would be weak, that he would fail . . . as we all do. We frequently don't stand for the Lord as we should—that's because we have the same competing loves in our

---

6. The Lord also spoke with Peter privately on at least one other occasion before He was seen by the rest of the disciples. Although we aren't given information about the discussions they had, it is easy to surmise that Peter's denial and Jesus' restoration of him were the topic (see Luke 24:34; 1 Cor. 15:5).

hearts that he did. We're afraid that others will censure us, that they will make fun of us or persecute us. We're ashamed of our inability to save anyone. We're just like Peter, aren't we?

In the midst of this sad reality is the joyous truth that because Peter was His, he would eventually prevail, that his faith would not fail utterly. This wasn't because of any inherent strength or faith on Peter's part. That's obvious, isn't it? Peter's faith would endure and grow through his failure because the Lord had prayed for him (Luke 22:32). You can comfort your heart with the truth that He also prays for you.

> Therefore He is able also to save forever those who draw near to God through Him, since He always lives to make intercession for them. (Heb. 7:25)

One Puritan wrote, "If you heard Christ pray for you, would it not encourage you to pray, and persuade you that God would not reject you?"[7] Even though we fail, even though we worship other gods, we can rest in the truth that God does save us forever. That's because the Lord Jesus is praying for us, and we know that His prayers, always in accord with God's will, are always heard (John 11:41–42). Yes, we may fail to stand as we should, to worship God alone, but because He is praying for us we will never fall from His loving grasp.

In our struggle against idolatry, let's learn to rest in the power of His prayer. As we continue to examine the influence of false gods, it will be important to remember that although you feel weak and vulnerable, God will strengthen you and keep you if you are His. The fact that you struggle with competing loves is no more of a shock to the Lord than Peter's denials were. But God sustained Peter

---

7. Baxter, *A Christian Directory*, 68.

during his fall, and He will sustain you. And the mere fact that you are struggling against them means that you are, in fact, His.

Whom Do *You* Worship?

In this chapter, I've tried to help you look a little more closely at the implications of the words, "You shall have no other gods before Me." At first blush it might have seemed that you were doing pretty well obeying this commandment. Perhaps now though, as you've looked into the lives of Martha, Eli, Abraham, and Peter, you may see areas in your life where other gods rule your heart. Can you discern where you worship, honor, trust, or love anything more than God? If so, don't despair. Remember that Jesus knew that Peter would deny Him, but because of His prayers Peter's faith continued to live and grow and be a blessing to others. I take great solace in Peter's denial, because I know that in all the ways that I've denied the Lord, He's praying for me and challenging me to focus my love wholeheartedly on Him.

In the next chapter, we'll look at the first commandment in greater depth and examine the place of the law in our lives as believers. For now, though, ask the Holy Spirit to quicken your understanding of your competing loves and gods.

FOR FURTHER THOUGHT

1. Refer back to the Westminster Larger Catechism answer (p. 38) and write out the verbs used to illustrate undivided worship. Underline those verbs that are meaningful to you.

2. As you consider the lives of Martha, Eli, Abraham, and Peter, what truths do they teach you about wholehearted worship?

3. Which of these people are you most like? Where do you find yourself failing?

4. What does the truth that Jesus is praying for you mean?

5. In *No God But God*, Os Guinness and John Seel state, "For followers of Jesus Christ, breaking with idols and living in truth are not a test of orthodoxy, but of love."[8] What do you think they mean?

6. Who or what competes most strongly for your love? Think about your relationships with parents, spouses, children, employers, and friends.

---

8. Os Guinness and John Seel, eds., *No God But God* (Chicago: Moody Press, 1992), 216.

3

Of First Importance

So then, the Law is holy, and the commandment is
holy and righteous and good. (Romans 7:12)

"You must leave this place right now! Don't bother to take
anything with you—just run away from the city before God's
wrath falls!"

Who were these strangers whom her husband had pro-
tected during the night? And what were they talking about?
Lot's wife wondered. *Why should we listen to them? Who do*
they think they are, telling us to leave our home? Perhaps this
is just another one of Lot's practical jokes.

"Can't we stay for a little while, Lot?" she begged her
husband. "You know, the girls' fiancés aren't convinced
that we need to go, so why don't we stay a little while longer to wait and see what happens? Perhaps we don't really
need to leave. I know that this city has problems, but what
city doesn't? Besides, you have a lot of authority here, and
maybe you can convince the people to change. Let's not do
anything rash."

Then, as the sun rose, an even more alarming event
took place. The two strangers forced her family out of the
city gates and ordered them to flee.

"Escape for your lives!" they warned. "Don't look behind
you! Don't stay anywhere near this city! God's punishment is

about to fall on this place, but He will protect you. Run! And remember, don't even take a moment to look behind you!"

As Lot, his wife, and their daughters fled from their home, Lot's wife felt a tug on her heart.

How can I leave my nice home, my dear friends, my fashionable city, my sphere of influence? I didn't even have a chance to take my beautiful pottery with me. What about my daughters' fiancés? I really don't want to leave this city—I love it, and I'll miss it so. The thought of leaving is so hard, and besides that, God knows I need my home, my dear home. I wonder if God will spare it. . . . I wonder what's happening to it. Lot is running on ahead—he'll never know if I steal one quick glance. I just need one last memory that I can carry with me . . . just one precious remembrance.

As Lot's wife turned around, she may have been transfixed by the awesome sight of molten fire raining down from heaven upon her city, her home. In that single instant, before she knew it, she was overcome by sulphurous vapors and encrusted with salt. The last view she had of her beloved world was of God's judgment of it.

Sometimes a simple action can speak volumes about character. In this case, a glance revealed a heart. Sodom was where Lot's wife lived physically, but it was also where her heart resided. She loved it, and her idolatrous heart clung to it because that was where her treasure was. Remember Jesus' words, "where your treasure is, there your heart will be also" (Matt. 6:21)? There was something in Sodom that she valued, esteemed, cherished, and loved more than she treasured God.

I live in the north county of San Diego, and as I look out over my lovely back yard, I can honestly say, "I really love where I live." God has blessed our family with a nice home in a pleasant part of the world. There's nothing sinful in enjoying and being thankful for what God has provided. In fact, it would be sinful not to enjoy His blessings. The problem occurs, however, when I love my home more than I love Him. If I treasure my nice home in the place of treasuring Him, then I've become an idolater. It's not wrong to thank God for His blessings, but when His blessings become our god, then we've fallen into idolatry. That was Lot's wife's problem: she treasured Sodom more than she treasured God. Jesus warns us to "remember Lot's wife" (Luke 17:32).

Are you beginning to see how your actions, like the actions of people in the Bible, reflect the focus of your love and worship? It's easy to see how Lot's wife had other gods, isn't it? It's obvious that she loved her city, wicked as it was. We can know that because she was willing to disobey God in order to sneak one last glance.

We need to grow in our understanding of the Scripture's teaching on idolatry, so we're going to consider God's explicit commands forbidding it. In doing so, I hope that you'll be able to see more clearly other gods you might have. In the process you'll learn that disobedience springs from the worship of other gods.

The Foremost Commandment

When Moses returned from meeting with God, he had with him God's instructions for life and worship in the form of Ten Commandments. God had given His children laws, showing them how to "fear the LORD . . . to walk in all His ways and love Him." He had commanded them "to serve the LORD your God with all your heart and . . . soul, and to keep the LORD's commandments . . . for your good" (Deut. 10:12–13).

Obeying God's commands is good. It is primarily good because it honors and glorifies God. James writes that the man who abides by the perfect law "will be blessed in what he does" (James

1:25). God has given us commandments about idolatry for our good . . . so that we will glorify Him and live lives marked by His good countenance upon us. Let's look now at the passage of Scripture that contains the first commandment, remembering that obedience to it is for our good.

I Am the Lord God

I am the LORD your God, who brought you out of the land of Egypt, out of the house of slavery. You shall have no other gods before Me. (Ex. 20:2–3)

As you can see, the first commandment includes the command, "You shall have no other gods before Me," and two reasons why we should obey the command. The first reason that God gives us is, "I am the LORD your God." God commands us to worship Him because He is God. You know, when we get down to it, that's the only reason we need. He deserves our worship because He is God. End of story. It is reasonable to worship Him as God simply because He is God and there's no one else like Him. "Thus says the LORD . . . 'I am the first and I am the last, and there is no God besides me. Who is like me?'" (Isa. 44:6–7).

Now, here's the really amazing part! He is not just *a* God or even *the* God, but He is *our* God. Not only is He totally above us, being eternal and unchangeable, the almighty, sovereign King; He's also near us—He's *our* God. He's condescended to fellowship with us and enter into a covenant of relationship with us. He is not just a King. He's also a Father, as Isaiah wrote: "For thus says the high and exalted One . . . whose name is Holy, 'I dwell on a high and holy place, and also with the contrite and lowly of spirit'" (Isa. 57:15).

He Brought Us Out
of the Land of Egypt

As if this weren't enough, God gives us another reason to direct our hearts to worship Him alone. This gracious, perfectly holy King brought us to Himself. It would have been right for Him to demand our worship because He is God. But that's not what He's done. He's "brought us out of the land of Egypt, out of the house of slavery." Before He demands His rightful worship He demonstrates His love and goodness toward us. Those of us who are His children have been set free from terrible bondage to sin, to Satan, and to death. He's done this for us! And now we must remember how He loved us and freed us, initiating relationship with us first. This is what John the Baptist's father said, "that we, being rescued from the hand of our enemies, might serve Him without fear" (Luke 1:74).

We've been rescued from the hand of our enemies so that we might serve Him. We've been set free from a land of idols so that we might worship Him. Every time Moses appealed to Pharaoh to let God's people go, it was so that they might serve Him. God wasn't releasing the Israelites from slavery so that they could join Club Med, though that's how many of them acted. He set them free so that they would celebrate, serve, and worship Him. His gracious work to free them was to ensure their hearts that He was trustworthy and filled with love for them. It was on this truth—His prior actions on their behalf while they were mostly unbelieving and filled with complaints—that He was to grant them faith to believe that they really were loved and He really was trustworthy.

We, too, have been set free from spiritual Egypt so that we can celebrate, love, and worship Him. When you think about the first commandment, do you remember His love toward you? Do you remember that even when you were His enemy He sent His Son to die in your place and free you from slavery? Remembering these things makes obedience more reasonable, doesn't it?

The First Commandment

God's primary command is, "You shall have no other gods before Me" (Ex. 20:3). How astonishing! By it, God demands our absolute and unequivocal devotion to Him alone. Only the "high and exalted One Who lives forever, whose name is Holy" has the right to demand such fidelity.

This commandment is preeminent because it is impossible for us to obey any of the other nine if we fail to obey this one. Every part of our devotion, every act of obedience or disobedience, every thought, word, and deed, hang upon our adherence to this command. You might be thinking, "Wow, that's a pretty sweeping statement," but think with me for a moment as we review a few of the other commandments:

- *"Honor your father and your mother."* Don't children fail to honor their parents because they have other gods such as their friends or the love of the world?
- *"You shall not murder."* Whenever someone takes the life of another, isn't that person saying, in essence, "I'm god. I can decide who will live and who will die"?
- *"You shall not commit adultery."* Isn't the taking of another's spouse the worship of another god such as romance, excitement, power, or pleasure?
- *"You shall not covet."* Strongly desiring anything that belongs to someone else is idolatry because it is the treasuring of something more than God and His will.

As you can see, having "no other gods" is the hinge upon which our entire obedience hangs. That is because the command against idolatry is really a command to love, to "hang our hearts" on God alone.[1]

"To say that there is one God and no god but God is not simply an article in a creed. It is an overpowering, brain-hammering, heart-stopping truth that is a command to love the only one worthy of our entire and unswerving allegiance."[2] The sum of this commandment is that we must set God apart from everything else in our hearts and give Him a place of priority above all else. It means that by faith we are to seek to believe that He is as good and loving as He claims to be and that He will be to us the source of all good, all our joys.

Perhaps now you have some general questions about the place of the Old Testament law in our lives.

The Ten *What*?[3]

For much of my Christian life, I was confused about the role of the Old Testament law. In particular, the Ten Commandments hung out there in my knowledge of the Bible something like the stories in the Old Testament. Yes, they were there. They seemed like they should be pertinent. And, yes, I supposed that I ought to obey them. But, honestly, I don't think that I ever thought very deeply about them. After all, they weren't all that important, were they? As a Christian, I had been taught that I wasn't "under the law" (whatever that meant), so why should I bother? I knew that my salvation was by grace alone—I didn't need to

---

1. Albrecht Peters, *Ten Commandments: Commentary on Luther's Catechisms* (St. Louis, MO: Concordia Publishing House, 2009), 106.
2. Os Guinness and John Seel, eds., *No God But God* (Chicago: Moody Press, 1992), 206.
3. For a discussion on legalism, see Appendix B.

obey the commandments to secure my right standing before God, and so, in some ambiguous way, I paid lip service to them and hoped that they would stay right where they were, back in antiquity.

The Use of the Moral Law for the Christian

Since that time, however, God has graciously helped me to learn that the law, as it is summarized in the Ten Commandments, does play an important role in the lives of Christians. The law teaches us the truth about our imagined goodness and the only sure way to heaven. Beholding God's unchanging standards in the Ten Commandments helps us to grasp the truth that no mere human has ever perfectly kept the law. Romans 3:23 says, "All have sinned and fall short." That's important for us to understand, because people trust that they are going to go to heaven because they're relatively good. Not unlike Patrick Swayze's character in the hit movie *Ghost*, modern man has created his set of standards that sound something like this: I'm pretty good. I'm not hurting anyone. I'm just doing my job, loving my girlfriend. Why, if anyone should go to heaven, it should be a nice fellow like me.

True Christians disagree with Hollywood's version of salvation. We believe something very different about how to attain it. We believe that people are unable to live a life that will satisfy God's perfect standards. That's because God is so holy and perfect that disobedience in just one area condemns us as lawbreakers. That's what James meant when he wrote, "For whoever keeps the whole law and yet stumbles in one point, he has become guilty of all" (James 2:10). Only one person has ever kept the law: the Lord Jesus Christ. Salvation is ours only through faith in the perfect law keeping of Jesus Christ on our behalf.[4]

4. If you aren't sure whether you're a Christian, please turn now to Appendix C, "How You Can Know If You Are a Christian."

The law helps me by serving as a tutor[5]—a personal teacher residing in the classroom of my heart, helping me to understand that I don't possess any innate goodness. It's easy for me to ignore God's law and compare myself with others—as I did in Asia! When I do, I always come to the conclusion that I'm pretty good. But if I examine myself in God's mirror (the perfect law),[6] I find that I am failing in every conceivable way.

The law humbles me and brings me to the end of my self-righteousness. As Paul writes, "I would not have come to know sin except through the Law" (Rom. 7:7). It forcefully shows me that I'm not deserving of salvation because I don't obey the Ten Commandments. Of course, since Phil and I have been married, I've never actually committed adultery outwardly, but the Law isn't merely concerned with outward obedience. As Jesus taught in the Sermon on the Mount, the Law must be obeyed inwardly as well . . . and if that's the standard, I've broken every single one of the commandments time without number. I have nothing for which to commend myself before a completely holy God. Counterintuitively, that's a good place for my soul to be in because it causes me to throw myself wholly on His mercy to me through Christ. It strips away my illusions of goodness and helps me to see how much I am in need of God's forgiveness.[7]

5. "Therefore the Law has become our tutor to lead us to Christ, so that we may be justified by faith" (Gal. 3:24).

6. "For if anyone is a hearer of the word and not a doer, he is like a man who looks at his natural face in a mirror; for once he has looked at himself and gone away, he has immediately forgotten what kind of person he was. But one who looks intently at the perfect law, the law of liberty, and abides by it, not having become a forgetful hearer but an effectual doer, this man will be blessed in what he does" (James 1:23–25).

7. Even though the law helps me to see my sinfulness, it's by God's mercy that I never fully see what God sees. I am unable to deeply comprehend how sinful my heart is, although the law does help me get enough of a glimpse of it to accomplish His purpose. "For now we see in a mirror dimly, but then face to face; now I know in part, but then I will know fully just as I also have been fully known" (1 Cor. 13:12). Let's thank God that we don't see face to face right now. Let's thank Him that we don't get the full picture of our sinfulness now, for I fear that our hearts would despair.

The law shows how much I desperately need Christ's perfect record applied to mine. That transfer of His record of complete obedience to mine, that imputed righteousness called *justification*, is the only hope I have, but it's all the hope I need.

The law teaches me how thankful I am to be for Christ's perfect keeping of it.[8] I am bound to Christ because He kept the Law perfectly, then bore the punishment for my lawbreaking in His body. By this my heart is prompted to overflow with love and obedience. As I compare my lawless life with His perfections, I am overcome with gratitude. And now, because of His work, I recognize that the requirement of the law is fulfilled in me[9] because I have His perfect righteousness. Isn't that incredible? As Christians, the requirement of the law is fulfilled in us!

The law becomes the standard of righteousness that I seek to obey out of gratitude. Like a thankful child seeking to please a favored parent, I have a desire for holiness that wells up out of a heart filled with thanksgiving. The law no longer condemns me, because I have been given the perfect record of Christ. Instead, as I grasp the truth of my utter dependence on His mercy, the law causes me to see my sin and long for His character in my life. I desire to

---

8. Westminster Larger Catechism,

Q: 97: What special use is there of the moral law to the regenerate?

A: Although they that are regenerate, and believe in Christ, be delivered from the moral law as a covenant of works,[1] so as thereby they are neither justified [2] nor condemned;[3] yet, besides the general uses thereof common to them with all men, it is of special use, to show them how much they are bound to Christ for his fulfilling it, and enduring the curse thereof in their stead, and for their good;[4] and thereby to provoke them to more thankfulness,[5] and to express the same in their greater care to conform themselves thereunto as the rule of their obedience.[6] l. Rom. 6:14; 7:4, 6; Gal. 4:4–5; 2. Rom. 3:20; 3. Gal. 5:23; Rom. 8:1; 4. Rom. 7:24–25; 8:3–4; Gal. 3:13–14; 5. Luke 1:68–69, 74–75; Col. 1:12–14; 6. Rom. 7:22; 12:2; Titus 2:11–14.

9. "For what the Law could not do, weak as it was through the flesh, God did: sending His own Son in the likeness of sinful flesh and as an offering for sin, He condemned sin in the flesh, so that the requirement of the Law might be fulfilled in us, who do not walk according to the flesh but according to the Spirit" (Rom. 8:3–4).

be holy because I love Him and want to be like Him. My righteousness is secure in Christ's perfect obedience for me, and by His grace, I am becoming "zealous for good deeds" (Titus 2:14).

The first commandment is primarily interested in my inward devotion: in it I am commanded to "love, fear, and trust in Him above all things."[10] Every sin, every idolatry in my heart, is rooted in lovelessness, thanklessness, and misplaced trust. Every time I worship something or someone other than God I forget that He's a good Father and a great King who has brought me out of Egypt. By contrast, every truly godly act, including even the inner desire to be godly, springs out of the love[11] and worship that He has placed in my heart. His grace causes me to delight in the law because I see it as the pattern for me to grow to be like Him. It was in this light that Paul said he "joyfully [concurred] with the law of God in the inner man" (Rom. 7:22). Because the Law can no longer condemn me, I no longer fear its accusation or resent its intrusion.

Yes, the moral law as summarized in the Ten Commandments is a wonderful gift.[12] We should look at it as "ten friends to guard our ways."[13] It humbles and convicts us, it fills us with thankfulness for our Savior's meek obedience, and it prompts us to live a life that will please Him:

> Walk in a manner worthy of the Lord, to please Him in all
> respects, bearing fruit in every good work and increasing in the

---

10. Martin Luther, "The Small Catechism," *The Book of Concord: The Confessions of the Lutheran Church*, accessed September 15, 2015, http://bookofconcord.org/smallcatechism.php.

11. "Because the love of God has been poured out within our hearts through the Holy Spirit who was given to us" (Rom. 5:5).

12. I want to distinguish the moral law (such as is contained in the Ten Commandments) from the ceremonial law (such as was used in the temple worship) and the civil law (which was written for the nation of Israel).

13. Ernest C. Reisinger, *Whatever Happened to the Ten Commandments?* (Carlisle, PA: Banner of Truth Trust, 1999), 13.

knowledge of God . . . joyously giving thanks to the Father, who has qualified us to share in the inheritance of the saints in Light. For He rescued us from the domain of darkness, and transferred us to the kingdom of His beloved Son, in whom we have redemption, the forgiveness of sins. (Col. 1:10–14)

The Finger of God

Remember with me those startling words that describe the initial giving of the law: "He gave Moses the two tablets of the testimony, tablets of stone, written by the finger of God" (Ex. 31:18).[14] The Lord God of all creation, the King of the heavens and the earth, wrote the law with His own hand![15] Isn't that incredible? But, as startling as that is, His never-ending compassion doesn't stop there. Ezekiel and Jeremiah foretell even greater mercies.

Moreover, I will give you a new heart and put a new spirit within you; and I will remove the heart of stone . . . and give you a heart of flesh. (Ezek. 36:26)

I will put My law within them and on their heart I will write it. (Jer. 31:33)[16]

---

14. In the recounting of the law, Moses wrote again, "The LORD gave me the two tablets of stone written by the finger of God; and on them were all the words which the LORD had spoken with you at the mountain from the midst of the fire on the day of the assembly" (Deut. 9:10).

15. Isn't the fact that God wrote the law with His own hand enough incentive for us to keep it?

16. It's interesting to note that God's writing of the law on our hearts of flesh will result in single-minded worship: "'But this is the covenant which I will make with the house of Israel after those days,' declares the Lord, 'I will put My law within them and on their heart I will write it; and I will be their God'" (Jer. 31:33); "Then I will sprinkle clean water on you, and you will be clean; I will cleanse you from all your filthiness and from all your idols. Moreover, I will give you a new heart and put a new spirit within you; and I will remove the heart of stone from your flesh and give you a heart of flesh" (Ezek. 36:25–26).

Amazing love! Whereas once God's law was written only on tablets of stone—standing outside us with external inducements to holiness and the power to condemn—now His law resides within our hearts, written by His hand! We are now impelled by an inward desire to obey Him without fear of condemnation for failure.

By His transforming power, God causes us to delight in His will. Our heart change has its origin in the joyful obedience of the Lord Jesus who delighted to do God's will because His law was in His heart. And now, in Him, God's law is written in our hearts, and we can begin to delight in it as well (see also Heb. 10:5–10).

It is because of these great mercies that we should seek to keep the commandments, remembering how He loved us and transformed us while we were His enemies.[17] In fact, a desire for obedience is the only sure evidence that we love Him; as John 14:15 says, "If you love Me, you will keep My commandments" (see also John 14:21, 23–24; 1 John 5:2–3).[18]

This demonstration of loving obedience is far removed from the lethargic apathy and saccharine self-centered feelings that pass for the love of God that I see so frequently in my own life. We'll always battle against our sin nature, and our obedience won't be perfected until heaven, but the focus of our lives should be evidenced in a growing joy in obedience and submission. Sometimes obedience and submission take the form of outward changes . . . at other times they are primarily concerns of the heart: Am I trusting in myself, in my own goodness and power to save,

17. "For if while we were enemies we were reconciled to God through the death of His Son, much more, having been reconciled, we shall be saved by His life" (Rom. 5:10).

18. Notice how the phrase "those who love Him and keep His commandments" is reiterated in Deut. 7:9 and Dan. 9:4 (see also Deut. 10:12–13 and 2 John 1:6). The Lord said that those who were the true members of His family were those who did the will of His Father: "For whoever does the will of My Father who is in heaven, he is My brother and sister and mother" (Matt. 12:50). He says, "You are My friends if you do what I command you" (John 15:14).

or am I trusting in Him alone? In my experience, it's much easier to put on a form of outward obedience, to stop doing something I shouldn't do. But I find it very difficult to hang all the desires, hopes, and expectations of my heart on His promise to love me, and to believe that He has nothing but good for me.

Commands about Idolatry

Commandments against idolatry are such a dominant theme in Scripture that it would be almost impossible for me to point out every instance where they're found. So let me share a few with you to firm up in your thinking that even though this seems like an obscure topic, it's not.

Commands in the Old Testament

> Do not turn to idols or make for yourselves molten gods; I am the LORD your God. (Lev. 19:4)

> You shall not follow . . . any of the gods of the peoples who surround you. (Deut. 6:14)

> Let there be no strange god among you;
> Nor shall you worship any foreign god. (Ps. 81:9)

> Let all those be ashamed who serve graven images,
> Who boast themselves of idols;
> Worship Him, all you gods. (Ps. 97:7)

> Yet I have been the LORD your God since the land of Egypt; and you were not to know any god except Me, for there is no savior besides Me. (Hos. 13:4)

Commands in the New Testament

> Then Jesus said to him, "Go, Satan! For it is written, 'You shall worship the Lord your God, and serve Him only.'" (Matt. 4:10)

> I wrote to you not to associate with any so-called brother if he is . . . an idolater. (1 Cor. 5:11)

> Do not be deceived; neither fornicators, nor idolaters . . . will inherit the kingdom of God. (1 Cor. 6:9–10)

> Do not be idolaters, as some of them were. (1 Cor. 10:7)

> Therefore, my beloved, flee from idolatry. (1 Cor. 10:14)

> Now the deeds of the flesh are evident, which are: . . . idolatry. (Gal. 5:19–20)

> Therefore consider the members of your earthly body as dead . . . to idolatry. (Col. 3:5)

> Little children, guard yourselves from idols. (1 John 5:21)

Are you beginning to see how dominant a theme idolatry is in the Bible? In light of this, I find it very interesting that in broader evangelicalism, we hardly hear it mentioned at all. Of course, in some circles, particularly Reformed ones, idolatry is a common topic of conversation. But still, considering that it is the most discussed form of sin in the Bible, shouldn't we be hearing more about it? Let's pray that God will open our eyes to the importance of our worship and teach us how to focus our love and devotion entirely on Him.

Building on the Foundation of the Commandments

Now that we've spent some time looking at the law, let's remember three facts about it: it humbles us and forces us to run to Jesus; it makes us thankful for Christ's perfect keeping of it; and it shows us what gratitude really looks like. God has been unbelievably gracious to us in furnishing us with new, warm hearts upon which He has written His living truth. We know that we're unable to keep the law as a means of salvation, but we also realize that a desire to grow in obedience is part of what it means to be His loving child.

Lot's wife was an idolater, but her idolatry didn't begin when she turned around to look at the city she loved. Her idolatry began when she treasured Sodom more than God, when her heart was tethered to her former life as she had come to know and love it. Her idolatry caused her downfall. The Bible clearly warns us, time and time again, to focus all our love and devotion on Him—for our good. As we continue in our study, we can be confident that the Holy Spirit is working in us, changing us and causing us to long to become loving and obedient children. Let's ask Him to help us love Him and embrace His law as a dear and welcome friend.

FOR FURTHER THOUGHT

1. Write out the Ten Commandments.

2. What has been your attitude toward the Ten Commandments in the past? What is it now?

3. Review the passages about idolatry on pages 62–63. Which ones speak specifically to your heart? What have you learned by looking over these verses? Where can you grow?

4. In Romans 8:4 Paul wrote "that the requirement of the Law might be fulfilled in us, who do not walk according to the flesh but according to the Spirit." How is the requirement of the law fulfilled in you as a believer? How does this verse calm or assure your heart?

5. As you reflect on Lot's wife's demise, do you see any similarity between her sin and your love of the world? Do you think that her sin was idolatry? Why?

6. Spend time now asking God to help you grow in your appreciation and understanding of His commandments, particularly of the first one.

4

The Heart Changer

*If God would not give me a heart to love
Him, I would I never had a heart.*[1]

Life on the streets of Nain was hard. As a prostitute, the
lifestyle she had once embraced in anger, hopelessness,
and rebellion had become bondage and bitterness. Her life
was empty and futile, and the future seemed to hold nothing more than shame and cynical hatred. Even though she
was familiar with acts of "love," her heart had never known
real love before, a love that captivated her heart with its
purity.

Along with her general hopelessness, a gnawing
awareness of the futility of her life was growing within her.
She was beginning to understand that her choices never
eventuated in freedom or pleasure; rather she was being
crushed by a sense of guilt and impending doom. No one
had to tell her that she was condemned . . . Satan never let
her forget it for a moment. The things that used to bring
her pleasure—power over men, the pride of being different
from other women, and the reassuring jangle of coins in
her pocket, now seemed so foolish, so meaningless, so futile. From deep within her she sensed a mysterious change

---

1. Richard Baxter, *A Christian Directory* (Morgan, PA: Soli Deo Gloria Publications, 1996), 125.

in her heart. She was beginning to believe that there was hope even for her. Perhaps there was a God who would forgive her. Gradually she detected a longing to love and know the God she had heard about all her life, the God of Israel.

As she gazed out over the plain of Carmel to the hills of Nazareth in the distance, she recalled stories she had heard about a certain Nazarene, Jesus. It was He who had raised the grieving widow's son to life and had said, "Do not weep" (Luke 7:13). Do not weep. Would He speak these words to her also? Could He change her life too? Or was she too far gone to hope for forgiveness?

As she watched His interaction with the common people from the shadows, she saw that He welcomed them and taught them with gentle wisdom. As she saw Him with the religious leaders, she knew He wasn't like them. It was true that He loved and obeyed the law, yet He was humble and gentle. He seemed so different from all the other men she had ever known. The desire to get to know Him began to captivate her. Some said that He was the Messiah. She had seen Him befriend and eat with sinners . . . Would the Messiah do that? Could it be that she had been wrong about God her whole life? It seemed as though He loved the outcasts. But would He receive her? What would He say to a woman who had been so entrenched in such sin and shame?

This compelling desire to know and love Him became like an addiction in her heart. "How can I get near Him?" she wondered. "What present could I bring to prove my sincerity?" She felt that it would be wrong to go to Him empty-handed, so she took her most precious possession, an alabaster vial of perfume, and went to seek Him.

On the day that she chose to go to Him, she discovered that He was having dinner at Simon's house. She knew that this Pharisee despised and condemned her, but in spite of that, she still had to get near Him. She had to find a way to express the love she had come to have for the One who had said, "Do not weep." In spite of her fear and shame, in desperation she imposed on Him.

Luke writes poignantly about this encounter:

And standing behind Him at His feet, weeping, she began to wet His feet with her tears, and kept wiping them with the hair of her head, and kissing His feet and anointing them with the perfume. (Luke 7:38)

The woman who may have heard Jesus say "do not weep" to a widow who had lost her son brought a heart filled with tears of love and repentance to pour on His feet. Rather than telling her not to weep, Jesus graced her with the ability to weep righteously, to mourn over sin, to love Him. He gave her a warm heart of flesh— one that could receive and embrace His person, His law. He freed her from a life of shame and in her tears that washed His feet, she found her soul was being washed as well. He gave her the ability to kiss holiness, to humble herself before a pure man, to use her perfume in worship of the perfect Man who was God.

In spite of the response of the Pharisees, she who had been so lost in immorality was now lost in sorrow and joy for sins recognized and forgiven. It no longer mattered what anyone else thought. She loved the Lord and humbled herself before Him. Jesus knew that her actions were motivated by love—a love that could ignore disapproval and disdain—a love that was willing to adore Him at the cost of all she had. Jesus recognized this love of hers and said, "Her sins, which are many, have been forgiven, for she loved much" (Luke 7:47).

This immoral woman, whose name we don't know, found forgiveness at the feet of the One who would give Himself for her many sins. She turned from the gods of her former life by laying down her self-punishment, her desire for security, her proud independence, and her prized treasure: the alabaster vial of perfume. The Holy Spirit had already worked so strongly in her heart that she could boldly ignore the proud disdain and hatred of the religious leaders. She was finally free of the guilt and shame that had enslaved her for decades, and no one was going to stop her from loving her Liberator.

Can you see how all Christians are just like this woman? When our eyes are opened to His worth, our hearts, like hers, overflow with love. And then, together with her, our souls can swim to heaven through a sea of tears.[2] As we grow in seeing His love in forgiving us, everything else will fade in value. Who cares if others disapprove or accuse? What does it matter if we give up our earthly treasures? This woman poured out her perfume because Jesus had given her a new treasure: a cleansed heart and life and a relationship with Him. Once she wept in bitterness for her earthly sorrows; now she wept in joy for forgiveness of sins. Did she know that God was saving up these cherished tears in an alabaster vial in heaven (see Ps. 56:8)?

The Incomprehensible Power of the Holy Spirit

What power could cause an immoral woman like this to kneel in contrite repentance before a Man in the home of her enemy?

---

2. Thomas Watson, *The Doctrine of Repentance* (Carlisle, PA: Banner of Truth Trust, 1994), 28.

There is only one soul-changing power in all the world: the Holy Spirit. He works in mysterious yet profound ways, causing us to grow in godliness, making us desire to be holy even as He is. Remember, He is called the Holy Spirit, and His work will always produce a longing for holiness in His children.

The work that the Holy Spirit does is unique in all the world. There are plenty of self-help programs for becoming a motivated sales person, a great tennis player, a better speaker. But there is only one Agent who can make a person want to obey the Father, only one Person who can engender love for God in our hearts, and that's the Holy Spirit. It's His dynamic power at work in our lives that we're going to examine in this chapter.

As you progress through this book and the Lord speaks to your heart about areas of idolatry, you may want to refer to this chapter from time to time. Rather than feeling overwhelmed or condemned in any way, remember that in your own strength you don't have the ability to make yourself love the Lord wholeheartedly. So if you begin to despair, recall first that your record is already sealed in the courts of heaven: you are righteous. Next, recall that God is committed to changing you—and He can change anyone (this is proven by fearful Peter's courageously facing a martyr's death)!

How the Spirit Makes Us Holy

Teaching Us the Glories of Christ

During His last evening with His disciples, Jesus taught extensively about the work of the Holy Spirit. Part of this teaching was that the Holy Spirit labors to glorify Christ. "He will glorify Me, for He will take of Mine and will disclose it to you" (John 16:14). The primary job of the Holy Spirit is to teach us about our wonderful Savior.

Exactly how the Spirit broods over our hearts and enlightens us is a mystery, but we do know that He teaches us how wonderful our Lord Jesus is. Like a master artist, the Spirit paints an exquisite portrait of Christ's perfections upon the canvas of our souls, illustrating His love, mercy, wisdom, kindness, humility, holiness, sorrows, and sweet amiableness. If you've ever been taken up in joyous exaltation of the Lord Jesus and His wondrous life, that was the work of the Holy Spirit in you. If you've ever been overwhelmed with the loveliness of His character while hearing the Word preached or reading one of the Gospels, that was His work as well.

Embracing Christ's beauty and glory is essential, because worship is a product of love. As the Holy Spirit opens your heart to Christ's beauty, your love will grow. The false gods that used to entice will lose their power to tempt. The Spirit makes us God-lovers, teaching us that loving the most beautiful Person in all the universe is not only wise but also reasonable. C. S. Lewis described the lesser joys or false gods as "mud pies."

> We are half-hearted creatures, fooling about with drink and sex and ambition when infinite joy is offered us, like an ignorant child who wants to go on making mud pies in a slum because he cannot imagine what is meant by the offer of a holiday at the sea. We are far too easily pleased.[3]

I can see that I'm like that ignorant child who finds pleasure, albeit fleeting, in those things that are familiar, within my reach, and enjoyed by my senses. How would those trifles look were I

3. C. S. Lewis, *The Weight of Glory and Other Addresses*, quoted in John Piper, *Desiring God: Meditations of a Christian Hedonist* (Sisters, OR: Multnomah, 1996), 83.

gazing like John into heaven, seeing my Savior's face; were I serving Him in the city with no need of the sun?[4]

Showing Us the Cross

The Holy Spirit was sent to convince the world concerning three things: sin, righteousness, and judgment (John 16:8–11).

Conviction of sin. The Spirit powerfully convicts the world about the sin of unbelief. This conviction is felt even by Christians who already believe that Jesus is God. The Holy Spirit brings conviction when we doubt the significance of Christ and His atoning work in our daily lives. Yes, we may reason in our Christian skepticism, perhaps Christ was God, and perhaps He did die for sin. But what does that have to do with God's ability to satisfy us and bring us peace today? Does He really forgive *all* my sin? Does He really still love me?

The sin of unbelief lies at the heart of all other sins and particularly at the heart of idolatry. "Idolatry is the most comprehensive description of the shape of unbelief used by the writers of the Bible."[5] It's easy to see why. When we fail to believe the truth about who Jesus is and what He has done in living perfectly and suffering and dying for our sin, it will be impossible to resist the allurement of the gods of this earth as they whisper their promised pleasures to us.

Believing and embracing Christ's atoning death for your sin is a fundamental key in abandoning the gods of this world. Do you sincerely believe that He died for your sin? If so, then is it logical to

4. "There will no longer be any curse; and the throne of God and of the Lamb will be in it, and His bond-servants will serve Him; they will see His face, and His name will be on their foreheads" (Rev. 22:3–4).

5. Os Guinness and John Seel, eds., *No God But God* (Chicago: Moody Press, 1992), 30.

think that He wouldn't grant you all you need? "He who did not spare His own Son, but delivered Him over for us all, how will He not also with Him freely give us all things?" (Rom. 8:32).

How desirable would those mud pies look were you standing before the cross, seeing the hands and feet that were pierced for you? Causing you to experience this truth is the work of the Spirit as He shows you the beauty of the cross.

Conviction about righteousness. The Holy Spirit also convicts us about Christ's righteousness and how He has gifted all believers with His perfect record. The Jewish religious leaders had accused Christ of being a heretic, and His death as a criminal seemed to confirm their words. But because of His resurrection and ascension into heaven, the Spirit now enlightens men's hearts to the truth that no matter how the world might rail against Him, Christ was perfectly righteous, and His righteousness belongs to all who believe.

It is particularly important for us to contemplate Christ's perfect nature because idolatry is always an assault against the character of God. Every time our hearts turn toward the worship of false gods, we're saying, "God isn't really good. He's not righteous. He's not loving or holy. I have to find other gods who will satisfy me because Jesus either can't or won't."

If you believe that Jesus is the perfectly righteous Son of God who is ruling from His Father's right hand, that's the Spirit's work. He will guard your heart against the lie that righteousness can come from any source other than Christ. He will guard you from believing that you have to gin up your own righteousness in order to be acceptable. In His role as the ascended Lord, He's already granted us all we need for righteousness and eternal happiness, and He is ruling in us to protect that inheritance (1 Peter 1:3–4). How would our idols appear were we gazing, as Stephen did at his death, into heaven where the ascended King was standing awaiting us (Acts 7:55–56)?

Conviction about judgment. Finally, the Spirit convicts us about God's judgment of sin and the certainty of sin and death's destruction. He has already judged sin powerfully in the cross by fulfilling all the Law in our place and dying the shameful death we deserved.

The Lord Jesus judged the "ruler of this world," Satan, by refusing to succumb to his temptations, by living a perfect life, and by wresting His Father's children out of Satan's hand by His death. God's punishment of the Devil will be fully complete at the end of time, when He has finished with him. But in the meantime, as you wrestle with the tragic effects of sin, you can take heart that God will be victorious over your soul's enemy. "The Son of God appeared for this purpose, to destroy the works of the devil" (1 John 3:8; see also John 12:31; Rom. 16:20; Col. 2:15; Heb. 2:14). Satan's power to accuse God's children and tell them of impending judgment and condemnation was swallowed up in the death of the obedient Son. All judgment for every believer's sin was poured into the cup He drank in love for us as He died in our place.

When you are tempted to think that the battle is lost and you might as well give up and serve other gods, plead with the Spirit to help you to know that your enemy is a condemned death-row criminal awaiting execution of his sentence (Rev. 20:10). There won't be any last-minute reprieves for him; no, just the certainty of God's fury and never-ending punishment. How would his lies about God's alleged defects or sin's supposed allurements, or his accusations of impending doom, appear if we saw him as he is: bound, under condemnation, and powerless outside God's sovereign will?

Writing His Word on Our Hearts

As we mentioned in chapter 3, the Holy Spirit writes God's law on our hearts. God's law now governs our lives internally, from our heart, as the Spirit helps us understand its meaning and applies it in our day-to-day lives. He teaches us what it means to take Him for our God and to be His covenant people (Jer. 31:33–34; 1 John 2:27).

This anointing from the Holy Spirit guides us into all truth (John 16:13). He teaches us so that we can come to know God as He is, rather than how we imagine Him to be. He doesn't want us to merely know about Him—He wants us to be intimately acquainted with Him. In our finite nature it's impossible for us to ever fully comprehend His person, but the Holy Spirit does grant a growing awareness of Him day by day. As we grow in understanding Him, His love, His trustworthiness, our bent to trust in other gods will diminish. That's how Paul could say that everything else paled in comparison with the treasure of knowing, comprehending, and understanding Him:

> More than that, I count all things to be loss in view of the surpassing value of knowing Christ Jesus my Lord, for whom I have suffered the loss of all things, and count them but rubbish so that I may gain Christ. (Phil. 3:8)

Why would Paul count everything he had—position, power, influence, and reputation—as garbage or, as the word *rubbish* is properly translated, excrement? Because the Holy Spirit had shown Him the character of Christ, and in comparison with that, everything that he had to offer by way of self-made goodness, everything the gods of this world offer, were good only for the dunghill.

Is He becoming that pearl beyond value that you're willing to sell everything else for? Is He worth pouring out your treasure for?

That's the Spirit's work in your heart. It's the Spirit's work to reveal the beauties of Jesus and His glorious Father to those who are His. "He will glorify Me, for He will take of Mine and will disclose it to you" (John 16:14).

Inclining Our Hearts to Worship Him

Without the work of God's Spirit, we'll worship everything—rather, anything—but God. He must work, then, to incline our hearts to worship Him.

At the dedication of the temple, Solomon prayed,

> May the Lord our God be with us . . . that He may incline our hearts to Himself, to walk in all His ways and to keep His commandments and His statutes and His ordinances. (1 Kings 8:57–58)

Solomon understood that the Holy Spirit needed to incline the hearts of his people to proper worship. That's because by birth we are naturally bent to worship the creation instead of the Creator. Without the intervention of God's Spirit, we're hopelessly doomed to invent false gods, to worship ourselves rather than Him. John Calvin wrote, "Daily experience teaches that flesh is always uneasy until it has obtained some figment like itself in which it may fondly find solace as an image of God."6

Solomon understood this, and that's why he prayed that God would incline the people's hearts toward Himself.7 God works by His Spirit to teach us that what once seemed like utter foolishness, a desire to love and trust in God alone, should be our chief

6. John Calvin, *Institutes of the Christian Religion*, ed. John T. McNeill, 2 vols., Library of Christian Classics (Philadelphia: Westminster, 1960), 1:108.

7. Although Solomon knew that God had to cause us to be God-worshipers, he fell into gross idolatry in his later life. One source of his idolatry was his pagan wives, who influenced his worship (see 1 Kings 11:5–10).

passion. It will be as we come to know Him in His kindness and love that we'll experience a freedom that engenders holiness. He does this by moving in our thoughts and affections. Under His tutelage we learn that ultimate goodness and joy are found in obedience and the single-minded worship of Jehovah. Solomon wasn't the only writer to mention the Spirit's power in moving us to holiness:

> Your people will volunteer freely in the day of Your power. (Ps. 110:3)

> For it is God who is at work in you, both to will and to work for His good pleasure. (Phil. 2:13; see also Pss. 51:10; 119:36–37; Jer. 32:39; 2 Thess. 3:5; Heb. 13:20–21)

Although the Spirit moving upon our inclinations might be a new concept, don't be discouraged; we'll look more closely at it later. For now, rejoice that the Holy Spirit changes us into God-lovers. That's why the Puritan Richard Baxter said, "If God would not give me a heart to love Him, I would I never had a heart."[8] God is willing and able to give His children hearts that love Him. Remember the immoral woman from Nain? If the Spirit can change her heart, He can change yours.

The Spirit Convinces Us That We Are God's Children

Another one of the Spirit's tasks is to convince us that we are members of God's family—that we're His children. For those who are sensitive to their sins, it is easy to doubt our adoption. When we begin to doubt, the next step is to turn away from our Father toward false gods or incessant works-righteousness. Grasping the

---

8. Baxter, *A Christian Directory*, 125.

truth that we're His is important because it will motivate us to worship Him. It will center our hearts. Paul writes about the Spirit's work in our adoption:

> You have received a spirit of adoption as sons by which we cry out, "Abba! Father!" The Spirit Himself testifies with our spirit that we are children of God. (Rom. 8:15–16)

Doesn't it endear God to you to know that you are His child? There is a great difference between worshiping a far-off god, some deity with whom you have no relation, and worshiping the God who also is your Father. The realization of His close relation to you should encourage you to focus all your love and devotion on Him.

The Spirit Teaches Us to Pray

Isn't it a blessing to think about all the ways that the Spirit enables us to become God-worshipers? As we struggle with our sinful idolatry, we'll frequently find ourselves in prayer for wisdom, strength, true hatred of sin, and love of righteousness. We need the Spirit's guidance even in our prayers. That's because, on our own, we don't even know how to pray. We don't know what we should pray for or even how to frame our desires. We don't know if our desires are idolatrous or if we're asking according to His will. It's in these times of deep, earnest prayer that the Holy Spirit will help us again.

> In the same way the Spirit also helps our weakness; for we do not know how to pray as we should, but the Spirit Himself intercedes for us with groanings too deep for words. . . . He intercedes for the saints according to the will of God. (Rom. 8:26–27)

What a precious thought! The Spirit aids us in our prayers. He helps us in our weakness. Instead of turning from us or refusing to hear our feeble cries, God sends His Spirit to aid us. He intercedes for us with our Father as we pray. The Spirit knows what our Father's will is, and He guides us in our prayers. Even when words are inadequate, He helps us by prayer "too deep for words." Think about how willing God is to help you, to aid you, to draw you to Himself, to free you from idolatry and make you know He's worthy to be loved. When we struggle with sin, we can know that the Spirit is perfectly framing our prayers for help. What a comfort the Spirit is to us!

God Is Faithful

In Paul's letter to the Corinthians, he reminded them of the folly of following Israelite errors and encouraged them to trust God's faithfulness.

> No temptation has overtaken you but such as is common to man; and God is faithful, who will not allow you to be tempted beyond what you are able, but with the temptation will provide the way of escape also, so that you will be able to endure it. Therefore, my beloved, flee from idolatry. (1 Cor. 10:13–14)

Paul sought to comfort them by reminding them that God's faithfulness can be counted on in time of trial and temptation. He wanted them to know that the temptation to idolatry is "common to man." They weren't alone in their struggle. He also wanted them to see that although the world and its false gods seem too powerful, "God is faithful." He won't turn His back on us as we struggle against our unbelief and sin. He'll carefully direct us so that we'll never encounter any temptation to idolatry that will be more than we can bear up against. And then He'll either make the temptation or trial disappear, strengthen us to resist it, or renew our faith if we fall. "There is no valley so dark but he can find a way through it, no affliction so grievous but he can prevent, or remove, or enable us to support it, and in the end overrule it to our advantage."[9]

It's in this light that Paul says, "Therefore, my beloved, flee from idolatry" (1 Cor. 10:14). God has promised to help you in your temptations and trials, especially as you see how He's loved you and how worthy of love He is. He's committed Himself to your holiness and to assisting you in glorifying Him.

The Certainty of Our Ultimate Glorification

The thought that I will one day be completely conformed to the glorious character of Christ is almost more than I can believe. But God has promised that the sanctifying work He's begun here on earth will ultimately be accomplished in heaven. Take heart in God's ability to change you:

> For those whom He foreknew, He also predestined to become conformed to the image of His Son, so that He would be the first-born among many brethren; and these whom He predestined, He also called; and these whom He called, He also justified; and these whom He justified, He also glorified. (Rom. 8:29–30)

Have you been called by God? Then you have been justified by Him. Have you been justified by Him? Then you will also be glorified by His power and changed into the image of His Son. Isn't

---

9. Ibid.

that remarkable? Because the Holy Spirit is faithful to complete all His work, we can be confident that God will somehow, by His great power and influence, cause us to reflect His character. He's begun this work now in this world, and He'll complete it in the next. It's in that knowledge that we can rest, assured of His continued love and guidance. As Joel Nederhood writes,

> Someday the glory of God's purity will be so shared with God's people that they will be like Jesus, perfect human beings as God intends them to be.[10]

Isn't the Spirit's influence precious? Does His commitment to obey the Father by comforting, changing, enlightening, and teaching you cause you to desire to cooperate with and rely on Him? Are you learning that you are so loved by Him that it's completely reasonable to want to love Him in return? That's how it should be. Remember, the Lord hasn't left you as an orphan. He's sent His Spirit to be with you and in you all through this journey.

In the next chapter we're going to be looking more closely at our pursuit of happiness and how that influences our choices of the gods we serve. But for now, take time to think about all the help the Spirit is to you in this battle and rejoice in Him.

FOR FURTHER THOUGHT

1. List each of the ways that the Spirit helps in the battle with sin and idolatry.

2. Which ones are most meaningful to you? Why?

---

10. Joel Nederhood, *This Splendid Journey* (Phillipsburg, NJ: P&R, 1998), 9.

3. Can you see any reason why the immoral woman Luke wrote about would turn to Christ? How could something so drastic happen?

4. How did the Spirit turn you to Christ? In what ways were the beauties of Christ and His cross made real to you?

5. How is idolatry an assault against God's character?

6. Calvin wrote, "The Word is the instrument by which the Lord dispenses the illumination of His Spirit to believers."[11] How has He used the Word to illumine your heart in this study? Are there any passages that are particularly meaningful to you?

7. Write out a prayer of supplication, asking the Spirit to help you even in your weakness to comprehend His role in your ongoing change toward godliness.

---

11. Calvin, *Institutes*, 1:96.

5

Better Than Life

Because Your lovingkindness is better than life,
My lips will praise You. (Psalm 63:3)

Sometime after the Lord sent Israel into slavery for idolatry, King Nebuchadnezzar set up a golden image in Babylon. He commanded all people to worship it whenever they heard the signaling music. For those who were idol worshipers, this image was just one more to add to their collection and nothing to fuss about. But for three Hebrew young men who had been taken from their homes as God's discipline for their parent's idolatry, the thought of worshiping the king's false god was abhorrent. It seems that Shadrach, Meshach, and Abednego had learned, "You shall have no other gods before Me."

"Is it true," the king demanded, "that you do not serve my gods or worship the golden image I have set up? . . . If you do not worship, you will immediately be cast into the midst of a furnace of blazing fire; and what god is there who can deliver you out of my hands?" (Dan. 3:14–15). This terrifying situation revealed these young men's hearts. Rather than acceding in fear or angrily blaming others, they simply replied,

> O Nebuchadnezzar, we do not need to give you an answer concerning this matter. If it be so, our God whom we serve is able to deliver us from the furnace of blazing fire; and He will deliver

us out of your hand, O king. But even if He does not, let it be known to you, O king, that we are not going to serve your gods or worship the golden image that you have set up. (Dan. 3:16–18)

These young men knew true happiness was not found in giving in to the demands of a pompous king—even if that king had the power and authority to take their lives from them. They understood that ultimate joy was to be found only in worshiping the living God. They were willing to sacrifice their lives to obey God and know His pleasure.

Why would obeying God seem so sweet that these young men would be willing to step into a fiery furnace? They had no guarantee God would deliver them from death. They were willing to die to avoid worshiping a false god. It's amazing the Holy Spirit could so work in them that they were convinced that death in faith was indeed better than an idolatrous life.

The Worth of God's Love

Think about David's words, "Because Your lovingkindness is better than life, my lips will praise You" (Ps. 63:3). I've sung the little chorus "Thy Lovingkindness" many times without ever thinking about it. Is God's steadfast love and mercy really sweeter to me than life? To answer that question, I'll replace the word *life* with more specific words like *wealth*, or *health*, or *a good name*, or *peace*.

- *Do I think that God's lovingkindness is better than a nice car?* Well, of course (unless my car won't start and I'm already late!).

- *Do I believe that it is more desirable than good health?* When I'm feeling well, yes. But when it's the middle of the night and I'm suffering, I wonder what I would do for a good night's rest.
- *Is His everlasting love more pleasurable than obedient children?* That question is a little harder because I believe that God wants my children to be obedient. But it would be easy to ignore God when dealing with an embarrassingly disobedient child.
- *Do I cherish God's lovingkindness as more precious than all else?* As I sit here, writing about Him, it's easy for me to answer in the affirmative. It's different, however, when I find out that my husband lost his job, my dearest friend is moving out of the state, or my computer has eaten two of my chapters. In those instances, I'm strongly tempted to forget about God's covenantal love if I think I can get what I want.

Is His love the greatest source of pleasure, happiness, or good? Does relationship with Him appear to be this sweet?

Man's Happiness Is God Himself

The Holy Spirit can make God your chief treasure. He influenced Saint Augustine to write, "Man's happiness is God Himself."[1] Like David, Augustine surveyed all that the world had to offer and said, *Nothing is better than knowing God. There is no pleasure greater than worshiping Him. Nothing is sweeter than His love. My happiness is found in Him alone.*

1. Thomas Watson, *The Ten Commandments* (Carlisle, PA: Banner of Truth Trust, 1995), 19.

Jesus' Happiness

In the wilderness, Satan tested Jesus along these same lines. *Is Your Father's lovingkindness better than life to You?* Satan offered Him "all the kingdoms of the world and their glory." "All these things I will give You," he said, "if You fall down and worship me" (Matt. 4:8–9). But Jesus refused to be an idolater. He so cherished God's love that when Satan offered Him all the pleasures of the world for His worship, He refused. Remember Jesus had just come from the waters of baptism where He had heard His Father's benediction: "This is My beloved Son, in whom I am well-pleased" (Matt. 3:17). Because the Lord knew that joy was found only in living in accordance with His Father's love, He was able to say, "Go, Satan! For it is written, 'You shall worship the Lord your God, and serve Him only'" (Matt. 4:10). Jesus knew the pleasure, the sheer joy found in fellowship with His Father. The covenantal love that existed between them was sweeter than anything Satan or the world could offer.

It was with thoughts of God's pleasure, "the joy set before Him" (Heb. 12:2), that Jesus endured the cross. How did Jesus bear that terrible night in the Garden of Gethsemane when His friends forsook Him and Judas betrayed Him? What drove Him on as He was beaten, mocked . . . as the crown of thorns was thrust into His head? What did He hold on to as He cried out in despair, "My God, My God, why have You forsaken Me?" (Matt. 27:46). What was so desirable that Jesus endured the cross and separation from His Father? Nothing less than the joy of knowing that He was pleasing to His Father by rescuing the bride He had been given. He would sit at His right hand for all eternity. On the cross Jesus proved that He valued God's lovingkindness better than life itself.

Peter knew this joy as he proclaimed, "You will make me full of gladness with Your presence" (Acts 2:28). David wrote of it: "In

Your presence is fullness of joy; in Your right hand there are pleasures forever" (Ps. 16:11). Along with our Savior, these men knew the joy that was more valuable and desirable than life itself.

I'm intrigued at the phrases "fullness of joy" and "pleasures forever." The Spirit opened David's eyes to something extraordinary—the pure ecstasy of unbridled fellowship with the most exquisite Being in all the universe. What joy would be ours if we could, for just one moment, wholly worship Him without any weakness, unbelief, or sin! What unspeakable pleasure will we know when we finally behold Him! Like David, we now say, "My soul thirsts for You . . . in a dry and weary land. . . . Because Your lovingkindness is better than life, my lips will praise You" (Ps. 63:1, 3). In heaven we'll be fully satisfied, filled with joy and pleasure. But can we taste this joy now? It seems some people have. And by His gracious will, we too will know moments of glory, moments when the joys of heaven seem almost tangible.

Delighting to Do God's Will

David prophesied of Jesus' desires. "I delight to do Your will, O my God," he wrote. "Your Law is within my heart" (Ps. 40:8). Jesus delighted in, enjoyed, and was enthralled by fellowship with His Father. He knew the sweetness that was a by-product of obedience and God-centered worship. And He lived His life in this obedience because He knew He was loved and cherished by the Father He loved to please.

Doing God's will was Christ's delight, and He was rewarded for it. "You have loved righteousness and hated lawlessness; therefore God . . . has anointed You with the oil of gladness" (Heb. 1:9). The Lord Jesus experienced great gladness, happiness of soul, because He loved righteousness and hated lawbreaking. He experienced the supreme pleasure of God's sweet countenance smiling down upon Him. He said, "He who sent Me is with Me . . . for I always do the things that are pleasing to Him" (John 8:29).

Delighting to do God's will means turning from the deception that joy can be found outside obedient fellowship with Him. We need to consistently question the imaginations that appear sweeter than God's lovingkindness. In order to do this, we'll have to be convinced that His presence is the loveliest treasure there is. We must believe that He'll lavish our lives with joy. "Is there not enough in heaven, in a life of endless joys with God, to make obedience lovely to you?"[2] Only the Holy Spirit can make Him look that good.

Can you say with Jesus, "I delight to do Your will, O my God"?[3] If so, that's the Holy Spirit's work in you. In all of the other areas where you still struggle with false gods and their lies, plead with Him to change your heart. He can cause you to long to serve Him, and you can rest in His mighty power, even when it seems that change is happening far too slowly.

Eve's Unhappy Choice

Let's consider sin's entrance into the world. "When the woman saw that the tree was good for food, and that it was a delight to the eyes, and that the tree was desirable to make one wise, she took from its fruit and ate; and she gave also to her husband with her, and he ate" (Gen. 3:6).

Why did Eve choose to disobey God? Look again at three words in the verse: *good, delight, desirable* are words that illustrate the motivation behind actions. Our choices are predicated upon what we think is "good," what we "delight" in, what we find most

---

2. Richard Baxter, *A Christian Directory* (Morgan, PA: Soli Deo Gloria Publications, 1996), 77.

3. Delighting in obedient fellowship is a recurrent theme in Scripture: Job 23:12; Pss. 40:8; 112:1; 119:11, 35, 47–48, 72, 92; Jer. 15:16; Rom. 7:22.

"desirable." The truth about our choices is that we always choose what we believe to be our best good. We always choose what we believe will bring us the most delight. When we sin it is always because we believe it is righteousness: choosing to be like God, reaching out and grabbing all the best. Sin never proclaims itself to be sin. It always masquerades as righteousness.

I'm not saying that we always choose what is morally good, for then there would be no sin, and we know that's not the case. What I am saying is that as we go through our day, we make choices based on what we believe is best—what we believe will bring us happiness. "The choice of the mind never departs from that which, at the time . . . appears most agreeable and pleasing, all things considered."[4]

Even though I purposely choose to disobey God (as Eve did), I always do so because I believe that's the best choice at the time. Eve thought that eating the forbidden fruit was her best, most delightful and desirable choice. She believed that disobedience was better than life. She was deceived into thinking it was righteousness. She forgot God's sweet lovingkindness. Sin is always occasioned in us by our belief in its goodness.

If you haven't thought about the reasons for choices you make, I know this might be confusing. Here are two simple analogies to illustrate this truth.

Get Fit!

Imagine the doctor says I need to start a regular exercise program so my bones will remain strong and my sleep will be sound. He tells me (and I believe him) that if I start exercising I'll feel better

---

4. Jonathan Edwards, *Freedom of the Will* (Morgan, PA: Soli Deo Gloria Publications, 1996), 13. John Owens concurs, "No choice is ever made without some degree of affection." James M. Houston, ed., *Sin and Temptation: The Challenge of Personal Godliness* (Minneapolis: Bethany House, 1996), xix.

and be healthier. I recognize that health is good, delightful, and desirable. I know that God wants me to care for my body. I determine that getting fit is a good in my life. I imagine how wonderful it would be to feel healthy, to be strong enough to go for a walk without panting—yes, being fit is good. So I decide that I'm going to choose to exercise.

The rub begins when I decide to go to the gym. I set my alarm for 6:00 a.m. My schedule is hectic, so I know I must get up early. But at 6:00 a.m. when my alarm rings, I can see another good: the pleasure of the warmth and comfort of my bed, the coziness of my blankets, the quietness of the house. All of a sudden something else appears more desirable to me—the good of staying in my warm bed, enjoying my solitude and rest. I can exercise tomorrow.

What seemed good in the early morning (staying in bed) was not good but had the appearance of it. I chose to stay in my bed because it seemed, at the time, the best choice. As I decided to pull the blankets up over my head, the option that appeared to hold the highest good for me, at the time, was the one I chose. I even told myself that it was good for me to rest more. Was it the best choice? Probably not. In the moment, lying in bed was enjoyable and seemed wisest, but if it had become habitual, I would have suffered the consequences. What appeared to be good was not, although it seemed good at the time.

Give Up!

We always choose what seems good, even when it is obviously evil. Imagine that I think the world would be better off without me. I start to consider suicide. Although it is difficult to imagine the goodness of my nonexistence, I begin to enjoy the thought. I take pleasure in thinking about others who would be sad at my death. I imagine how their lives would be better off if I weren't around. I dream about rest and freedom from my troubles. The more I contemplate the apparent goodness of my death, the more I long for it. All that stops me from killing myself is the good of self-preservation. Everything in me screams that the end of my existence isn't good, but I'm beginning to love and delight in the idea. If I commit suicide, I don't do so because I'm purposely choosing what appears evil, although I might know suicide is sin. I'm choosing what I believe to be the highest good: the end of all my troubles and ultimate freedom. To the person who commits suicide, death appears more pleasurable than life.

You might be wondering what all this has to do with the worship of false gods. Would you be surprised if I said, "Everything"? We erect false gods because we believe they can bring us happiness, our highest good.

Don't Say the "H" Word!

I'm going to speak about the goodness of pursuing happiness in this book. If you're like me, that might make you uncomfortable. It seems to me that many Christians struggle with the word *happiness*. I can understand that. As Christians serious about God's call to self-denial, we feel compelled to object to the easy, self-focused, self-absorbed religion that passes for Christianity in our culture. Let me say unequivocally that I agree with these concerns.

I reject the thought that God saved me so He could give me a new Cadillac. I refuse the belief that I am the center of the universe and that God exists to bring me whatever I want, when I want it.[5] I recognize God as the source and meaning of everything: the Sun of my orbit. I know my life was created to bring pleasure to Him. He is, as Paul writes, "God, the Father, from whom are all things and we exist for Him" (1 Cor. 8:6; see also Rom. 11:36; Col. 1:16).

5. Bob Dylan expresses this well in his song "When You Gonna Wake Up."

In my office is a Mary Englebreit poster, *The Queen*. It's a picture of a girl with crown, scepter, and sunglasses, smugly surveying her realm over a castle wall. The caption reads, "The Queen of Everything." A friend gave me this poster because we joke about being "the queen." The poster is funny because it strikes so close to home. Unless God teaches me otherwise, I believe I am the center of the universe, The Queen of Everything. Before we continue discussing the pursuit of happiness, let me state that I firmly reject man-centered philosophies. I must admit, however, that I still wrestle with my personal desire to be The Queen of Everything—or at least The Queen of My Own Little World.

Running after Happiness

Surprisingly, I first became comfortable talking about pursuing happiness through the writings of the Puritans. As I began to read them, I was struck by the number of times they used the word *happiness* in a positive light. What a shock it was to read of happiness from these men whom the world paints as grumpy, gloomy killjoys. For instance, Thomas Watson wrote, "[God] has no design upon us, but to make us happy," and, "Who should be cheerful, if not the people of God?" William Gurnall wrote, "To see a wicked man merry, or a Christian sad, is alike uncomely."[6]

The Puritans did not have in mind the shallow happiness experienced from temporal pleasures. They knew deep happiness was found in close relationship with God. It was available only to those who sought to be holy. "Those that look to be happy," Richard Sibbes wrote, "must first look to be holy."[7] Notice that

6. I. D. E. Thomas, comp., *The Golden Treasury of Puritan Quotations* (Carlisle, PA: Banner of Truth Trust, 1997), 158–59.
7. Ibid., 158.

he didn't say, "Don't look to be happy," but rather, "Seek your happiness where it really is—in holiness," in a life lived under the love of God. One Puritan prayed, "Thou canst not make me happy *with* Thyself, till Thou hast made me holy *like* Thyself."[8]

These writers knew it was in the nature of mankind to pursue happiness and that it would be fruitless to teach otherwise. They also knew that happiness could not be found other than in God, especially not in those worldly pleasures that "satisfy the deluded."[9] "Happy is that people . . . whose God is the LORD!" writes the psalmist, and the Puritans would heartily agree (Ps. 144:15 KJV).[10]

Pursue the happiness of knowing and loving Christ, resting in His love for you, and you will find that your holiness and worship will grow. You can pursue Him without fear of losing anything worthwhile, for "He will use you only in safe and honorable services, *and to no worse an end than your endless happiness.*"[11]

Why Do We Choose the Way We Do?

We disregard the first commandment because we have other desires and delights. What do you believe will make you happy? How do your desires affect your holiness? If I observed your life, what

8. Arthur Bennet, *The Valley of Vision: A Collection of Puritan Prayers and Devotions* (Carlisle, PA: Banner of Truth Trust, 1975), 93.

9. Ibid., 216.

10. In his introduction to *The Ten Commandments*, Thomas Watson writes page after page about the happiness and blessedness of knowing and loving God. He writes, "*God is the chief good.* In the chief good there must be delectability; it must have something that is delicious and sweet: and where can we suck those pure essential comforts, which ravish us with delight but in God. *In God's character there is a certain sweetness which fascinates or rather enraptures the soul*" (22, emphasis added). John Piper has also written eloquently about the appropriate pursuit of happiness in his wonderful books, beginning with *Desiring God: Meditations of a Christian Hedonist* (Sisters, OR: Multnomah, 1996). Piper recognizes that man will pursue happiness and encourages it. He sees that man can and should wholeheartedly pursue the joy that God experiences in fellowship with Himself. Piper says that pursuing happiness in God is the great business of life. He believes that God is most glorified by lives that reflect great happiness in knowing and loving Him.

11. Baxter, *A Christian Directory*, 75.

conclusions would I draw about the priority of God's love? Here are illustrations to help you begin to answer these questions.

Assume that you are habitually angry with your spouse. Ask yourself, "What good or happiness do I think I am missing? What is the delight or joy that I'm trying to get by acting this way?" Some answers to these questions might include, "I can't be happy without my spouse's respect. When I'm disrespected, I respond in anger." In this case, your spouse's respect is what you view as your highest good, your source of happiness. And since you're willing to sin to obtain it, it is also your god. Of course, wanting to be respected in appropriate ways isn't sinful in itself. It is just that when we believe that respect is necessary for our happiness, we're giving it (and others) too much power in our lives.

Or you might answer, "My spouse doesn't communicate the way I desire. I can't be happy without good communication. I act this way to try to get what I want." In this case, a spouse who communicates well is your highest good—your source of happiness. Remember that when you're willing to sin in order to be happy, this happiness (however you define it) is your god. Good communication is a blessing and a wonderful gift between people, but it isn't the key to ultimate happiness. Remember that we can make even good things into idols by wanting them too much or by investing them with too much importance.

Here's another example. Whenever you feel anxious, you go to the mall and spend money excessively. Ask yourself, "What good do I think I'm missing? What is the joy I get from spending money?" One answer might be "I long for a life free from concern. My life seems so difficult; I enjoy bringing pleasure to myself. Spending money brings me happiness." In this case, the ultimate good that you are pursuing is the pleasure of thinking of yourself as being able to buy whatever you want, whenever you want it.

The happiness that you experience when you put on new clothes or look at that furniture is your functional god because you are willing to sin to get it.

Here's one more illustration. You've just changed churches, and although you know that the Lord wants you to be involved with people, you bolt out the door immediately after the service. When you can't avoid staying, you keep yourself aloof. You tell yourself that you're shy and that it's hard for you to make friends. If this sounds familiar, ask yourself, "What is the happiness that I think I need? What is the joy that I think I'll get keeping myself isolated?" One answer might be "I need people to accept and love me. People have hurt me in the past, so now I don't give them a chance to reject me. Happiness is found in a self-insulated life." Perhaps the highest good or joy that you can imagine is feeling secure. Even though you know you aren't secure, at least you aren't being rejected, so you feel more in control. In this case, control and self-protection are your supposed highest good.

Your History and Happiness

As you look back over your life, you might be able to see why you believe the way you do about your personal highest good—your source of happiness. Perhaps you grew up in a home where everyone was treated with great respect, and you've come to believe that's necessary for happiness. Or, conversely, you might have watched a parent be disrespected, so you made a heart promise that you'll never be treated that way.

Possibly you watched a parent self-indulge whenever circumstances were falling apart, and you believe that's the appropriate way to handle stress. Or perhaps a parent was extremely self-disciplined, and you felt alone when life was frightening. Maybe you learned to long for pleasure during turmoil. Now you just think of yourself as being stressed or nervous.

The shy person may have grown up with a demanding parent or sibling who was never satisfied. He found that the best way to avoid the pain of rejection was to avoid taking a chance on relationships. Or maybe he grew up with an overly attentive parent who lavished him with so much love that he feels rejected when others don't respond in the same way. His habitual way of interacting with others has become ingrained, and now he thinks of himself as shy.

Our Unique Hearts

Can you see how every person has a unique heart that responds in uniquely different ways? Although we all have the same sinful nature and bent to create false gods, we create them for very different reasons. We create images out of our thoughts of our highest good or happiness. And whether we're aware of it or not, those images are the driving forces in our lives. They direct our worship, either toward or away from God. They tell us what we should cherish more than Him.

Sometimes we think that our personal history blocks us from worshiping God. But remember Shadrach, Meshach, and Abednego? Neither their childhoods nor present lives were pleasant. Perhaps their parents were idolaters who had been killed at the fall of Jerusalem. They were captives in a foreign country. But they had been taught by the Holy Spirit that even if it cost them their lives, there wasn't any greater joy than experiencing sweet fellowship with their Father. If He could teach these orphans that truth, He can do the same thing for you.

God can teach you that He is your highest good. He can show you that all your happiness is in Him. He delights in bringing His people face to face with the happiness that is His alone. You can pray,

> O Christ,
> All thy ways of mercy *tend to and end in my delight.*
> Thou didst weep, sorrow, suffer that *I might rejoice.*
> For my joy thou hast sent the Comforter,
> multiplied thy promises,
> *shown me my future happiness,*
> given me a living fountain.
> *Thou art preparing joy for me and me for joy;*
> *I pray for joy, wait for joy, long for joy;*
> *give me more than I can hold, desire, or think of.*[12]

The good news is that the Holy Spirit can illumine your heart and cause you to grow in your esteem of Christ and disdain for the charms of the world. He does this by inclining you to serve Him and teaching you the true joys of heaven. So, go ahead! Pursue happiness! Define it the way that God does and you'll never be disappointed. Remember your goal is to say with David, "Nothing, not even life, brings me more happiness than Your love!"

FOR FURTHER THOUGHT

1. What did Augustine mean when he said, "Man's happiness is God Himself"?

2. What do you think about the pursuit of happiness? In what sense would it be godly or ungodly?

12. Bennet, *Valley of Vision*, 162. Emphasis added.

3. Explain what it means to pursue your highest good. Does this mean that we always choose what is morally good? Why would something harmful, like suicide, seem good?

4. Think back to the last time you know you sinned. Ask yourself, "What was the good I wanted? What was the joy that I thought I'd get by pursuing this sinful course of action? How was sin masquerading as righteousness?"

5. What are the desires that appear to hold happiness for you? Completing the following sentence will help you to see what they are. "My life would be perfect if . . ."

6. What circumstances in your life taught you to hold certain things as your highest good? Do you believe that God can redeem circumstances and teach you to value Him as your happiness?

6

Knowing Your Heart

"Oh that they had such a heart in them,
that they would fear Me and keep all My
commandments always." (Deuteronomy 5:29)

Unlike the immoral woman of Nain, Rahab the harlot[1] had
never heard from her neighbors about the God of Israel.
All she had known was idolatry and prostitution. She lived
among a doomed people—a people upon whom God had
pronounced judgment.[2]

Rahab's home was conducive to her trade. There, on
the wall of Jericho, she could see travelers who might
be interested in a comfortable night's rest. From these
travelers she had probably heard that the people known
as the sons of Israel were headed her way. All her life she
had heard the stories about how the Egyptian army had
drowned in the Red Sea. She had heard what had happened to the kings of the Amorites who had been "utterly
destroyed" (Josh. 2:10). And now, these seemingly invinci-
ble people were headed toward her city.

As she entertained the Israelite spies, perhaps she
thought she might be able to exchange her life for favors,

---

1. If you're unfamiliar with the story of Rahab, see Joshua 2.
2. God had foretold Abraham of the Amorites' coming destruction: "Then in the fourth
generation they will return here, for the iniquity of the Amorite is not yet complete" (Gen.
15:16).

but these men were different. They weren't interested in her gifts—they seemed honest and devout.

As she interacted with the spies, she made a seemingly illogical choice. She chose to ally herself with them. This choice was illogical because Jericho was a strongly fortified city on a hill. With inner and outer walls eighteen feet thick, it had stood for years against attack. But Rahab, this idolatrous harlot, believed that her highest good lay in aiding her enemies' scouts. Consider the astonishing statement that Rahab made to the spies:

> I know that the Lord has given you the land, and that the terror of you has fallen on us, and that all the inhabitants of the land have melted away before you. . . . Our hearts melted and no courage remained in any man any longer because of you; for the Lord your God, He is God in heaven above and on earth beneath. (Josh. 2:9, 11)

How did she know that the Lord had given them the land? Well perhaps, you might reason, she was just hedging her bets. Perhaps she didn't know but thought it would be good to protect herself just in case. If that were true, why would she risk her life and lie when questioned about the men? How did she know the Israelite God was the true God? We don't know the answer to these questions, but we do know that God had revealed Himself to her heart in some way.

Rahab's history is one of the most delightful and amazing in the Bible. Without anything to recommend her—in fact, with everything to censure her—she became a favored woman. Rahab's story doesn't end with harboring the spies and escaping from Jericho. She eventually married Salmon, a leading Israelite, and became the mother of Boaz. Boaz married Ruth, and they gave birth to Obed, the father of Jesse. This man was David's father, through whose family Jesus was born.

Every Christian woman who has a checkered past can rejoice in the story of Rahab. We can be comforted that God chose her out of her doomed city, protected her, and ensured her safe escape when chaos reigned around her. Not only did God protect and deliver her, but he also delivered her family with her. What a blessed story! God taught her what she needed to know. He taught her that it was her highest good to hide the spies. He delivered her and gave her a family and a place of honor among all the women of faith in the world. She is one of only two women listed in the heroes of faith: "By faith Rahab the harlot did not perish along with those who were disobedient, after she had welcomed the spies in peace" (Heb. 11:31).

Rahab knew of God's conquering power because He had already informed her mind, conquered her heart, and birthed faith in her. This faith made her aware of His will and gave her courage to seek to be obedient to it. If God can so move on a Gentile prostitute's heart and give her faith, He can work in you too. He can instruct your heart and cause you to understand and desire truth.

In the previous chapters we've seen how the choices we make are based on estimates of our best chance for happiness. We've been encouraged to recognize that there is no happiness better than knowing God's unfailing love.

As we discussed the process of choice, perhaps you were curious about your ability to discern between true and false promises of happiness. You might have wondered how you could grow in your love for God and in your desire to pursue true joy. After all, those "mud pies" C. S. Lewis wrote about seem appealing, don't they? In the next few chapters, we're going to take a deep look at the functioning of our heart. We'll see how wholehearted devotion can begin to be developed. Remember that when Jesus gave the foremost commandment, He said that our whole heart, soul, and mind must be enraptured with God. When He said this, what did He mean? What was His understanding of the heart?

Understanding the Heart

When Jesus spoke of the heart, He was talking about the inner you. When the Bible refers to the heart, it means the three main operations of the inner you: your mind, affections, and will.

The Mind

The term *heart* refers first to your mind, which includes your thoughts, beliefs, understandings, memories, judgments, conscience, and discernment. Consider the following verses that illustrate this point:

I have given you a wise and discerning heart. (1 Kings 3:12)

The heart of this people has become dull . . . otherwise they would . . . understand with their heart. (Matt. 13:15)

But some of the scribes were sitting there and reasoning in their hearts. (Mark 2:6)

And He said to them, "Why are you troubled, and why do doubts arise in your hearts?" (Luke 24:38)

For even though they knew God . . . their foolish heart was darkened. (Rom. 1:21)

The goal of our instruction is love from a pure heart and a good conscience and a sincere faith. (1 Tim. 1:5)

As you can see, the Bible uses the word *heart* to speak about your ability to think, understand, doubt, reason, discern, and remember. This is different from the way we Westerners think of the term *heart*. We usually refer to these kinds of activities as being outside the heart, solely in the mind. We don't usually say, "I was thinking in my heart . . ." or, "I've made up my heart about it!" But, biblically speaking, the mind is just one of three areas of operation of the heart or inner person.

The Affections

Another part of our inner person or heart is what the Puritans would call "affections." Our affections include our longings, desires, feelings, imaginations, and emotions. This word is used in the way that we would normally use the word *heart* in our culture. When we say that we have a broken heart, we usually don't mean that our thinking is damaged or that our physical heart isn't pumping blood properly. What we usually mean is our feelings and longings are pained. The Bible presents a broader view of the heart, of which our feelings and desires are one function. Briefly, here's how the Bible refers to this area of our inner person:

Serve the LORD your God with joy and a glad heart. (Deut. 28:47)

The heart of the people melt with fear. (Josh. 14:8)

Why do you weep . . . and why is your heart sad? (1 Sam. 1:8)

May He grant you your heart's desire
And fulfill all your counsel! (Ps. 20:4)

The imaginations of their heart run riot. (Ps. 73:7)

Do not be eager in your heart to be angry. (Eccles. 7:9)

Follow the impulses of your heart. (Eccles. 11:9)

Say to those with anxious heart,
"Take courage, fear not." (Isa. 35:4)

For consider Him . . . so that you will not grow weary and lose heart. (Heb. 12:3)[3]

But if you have bitter jealousy and selfish ambition in your heart . . . (James 3:14)

As you can see, the Bible speaks of your heart as being the seat of your emotions, imaginations, longings, and desires. For our discussion, we'll use the Puritans' word, *affections*, when we talk about this aspect of our inner person because we want to consider more than just the emotions. It is particularly important for us to understand our affections because they are influential in worship.

The Will

The third way that our heart functions is the will. The will is the part of the inner person that chooses or determines what actions we take. The will is informed by the mind and the affections about the best course of action, and then the will acts upon it. Of course, our will is broken and enslaved. So it's important to remember that as we struggle to choose the right course of action, Jesus was the only human whose will was completely free, free to choose to serve His Father in every circumstance. Even after we come to the Lord

---

3. This is a verse that combines two areas of the heart's function: the mind (consider) and the affections (lose heart or become sad).

Fig. 6.1. A Biblical Portrait of the Heart

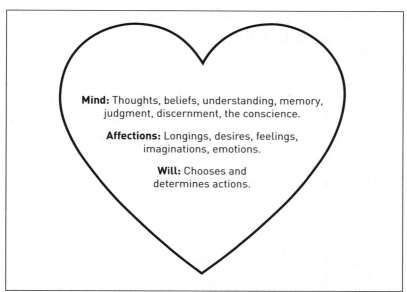

Mind: Thoughts, beliefs, understanding, memory, judgment, discernment, the conscience.

Affections: Longings, desires, feelings, imaginations, emotions.

Will: Chooses and determines actions.

and He regenerates us, our old nature will still struggle with freely choosing His good pleasure.

Choose life in order that you may live. (Deut. 30:19)

Choose for yourselves today whom you will serve. (Josh. 24:15)

He will eat curds and honey at the time He knows enough to refuse evil and choose good. (Isa. 7:15)[4]

Who is the man who fears the LORD?
He will instruct him in the way he should choose. (Ps. 25:12)[5]

4. This verse demonstrates the relationship between the mind instructing the will: He knew to choose good.
5. This is a verse that describes God's influence on the mind, teaching the will the right choice.

If you've never thought about your heart in this way before, perhaps this is a little confusing. Just remember that, biblically speaking, your heart functions in three different ways: the mind, the affections, and the will. Perhaps figure 6.1 will help clear up any confusion you might still have.

Rather than thinking about these three aspects (your mind, affections, and will) as being separate and isolated from each other, think of them as continually working in conjunction with each other. (Look back at Isaiah 7:15, Deuteronomy 23:15–16, and Psalm 25:12 for examples of this.) It is difficult to differentiate between them in our day-to-day lives. Think of them as you might think of your brain, your heart, and your lungs. As you are sitting here reading this book, you aren't aware of what part of your body is working to keep you alive. That's because every part is working together. It is true that if one part stopped working, you'd become aware of it pretty quickly. In normal circumstances, though, it's not something we think about.

In one sense, that's how our minds, affections, and wills operate. Your mind should inform your affections of the source of your highest happiness; your affections imagine it, cause you to long for it, and apply the impetus needed to awaken your will to choose. We never sit around thinking about whether it's our affections, minds, or wills that cause us to choose vanilla over chocolate ice cream. We just do it.

In Hebrews 11, all three aspects of the heart's function are referred to in one passage about Moses. See if you can pick them out.

> By faith Moses, when he had grown up, refused to be called the son of Pharaoh's daughter, choosing rather to endure ill-treatment with the people of God than to enjoy the pass-

ing pleasures of sin, considering the reproach of Christ greater riches than the treasures of Egypt; for he was looking to the reward. By faith he left Egypt, not fearing the wrath of the king; for he endured, as seeing Him who is unseen. (Heb. 11:24–27)

Look again at these verses. Do you see how Moses' mind, affections, and will each interacted with his faith? His mind regarded or considered disgrace as a greater happiness than the treasures of Egypt. His affections longed for the happiness that his mind judged would have greater value than the pleasures of sin. His imagination looked ahead and saw the reward that would be his. His mind informed his affections that this reward would bring him greater happiness than anything Egypt had to offer. Moses thought, felt, desired, and acted on his belief that disgrace for Christ would bring him greater happiness than pleasures in Pharaoh's house. And finally, his will was moved, and he "refused to be called the son of Pharaoh's daughter." By God's grace Moses believed that disgrace and deprivation for the sake of God's lovingkindness was better than a life of pleasure and power.

As you can see, Moses' heart (the mind, emotions, and will) acted together, directing his worship by discerning, desiring, and choosing which god he would serve. His heart was moved to right thoughts, feelings, and actions by his faith. He saw that there would be greater happiness in suffering for the living God than in a life of ease in Pharaoh's palace. When God eventually gave him the law on Mount Sinai, by faith he had already decided that Jehovah would be his God.[6]

---

6. God helped Moses along the way with his decision: He birthed faith in his heart, He caused him to notice his brothers, and He providentially allowed Moses to kill an Egyptian. Moses left Egypt because he had to; his choice was forced—all according to God's sovereign plan.

Our Heart Disease

"Well," you might be thinking, "if I could just direct my thinking toward God, learn to desire Him, and then choose Him, I'd be okay . . . right?" Well, yes and no.

Yes, it is true God does call us to learn and embrace the truth with our mind. He calls us to desire and long for Him with our affections. He commands us to choose Him with our will. He does hold us responsible in each of these ways. But we have a problem, don't we? Without God's grace, we'll never understand, desire, or choose Him. This truth is reflected in Augustine's prayer, "Give what thou commandest and command what thou wilt."[7] We can't accomplish this or any heart change on our own. We need His grace to teach, incline, and direct our hearts to Him. So, *yes*, as you by faith present your heart to Him for surgery, He will graciously cause you to grow in love for Him, particularly when you spend time considering how deeply He loves and consistently forgives you.

However, we have a major heart problem against which we will have to struggle our entire lives. There will never come a time when our heart will be completely conformed to loving and worshiping Him—at least not this side of heaven. Jeremiah spoke thus about our heart's disease: "The heart is more deceitful than all else and is desperately sick; who can understand it?" (Jer. 17:9). Our heart is false—it tricks or deceives us into thinking that our desires are pure, that we want what we want because it is good and God approves. Every man's way seems right in his own eyes . . . even when that way leads to death. Our heart trouble is hereditary: it had its origin at the fall. Ever since Adam, all people have had this problem—we all have a sin nature, as the Bible teaches:

7. Saint Augustine Bishop of Hippo, *The Confessions of St. Augustine*, trans. E. B. Pusey (Oak Harbor, WA: Logos Research Systems, Inc., 1996). Book 10, Chapter 29.

Every intent of the thoughts of his heart was only evil continually. (Gen. 6:5; see also Gen. 8:21)

Behold, I was brought forth in iniquity,
And in sin my mother conceived me. (Ps. 51:5)

The hearts of the sons of men are full of evil and insanity is in their hearts throughout their lives. (Eccles. 9:3)

As you can see, the heart or inner man is full of evil and deception. Jesus taught it is the fountain from which all our sinful thoughts, words, and deeds flow; it is the seat of our unbelief. Even though believers have been given a new heart so that our thoughts and desires are being changed, we still struggle with the remnants of our old nature. We must continually battle the competing loves in our hearts. Every day we have to choose whom we will love most: God or ourselves (and the gods we create). The difficulty of this choice is compounded because our hearts deceive us into thinking that acting in some sinful way is the best or perhaps the godliest course of action. Remember: sin never entices you as sin; it always comes to you dressed as righteousness.

Let me illustrate this for you. When the Pharisees spearheaded the movement to crucify Christ, they thought they were doing God a favor. Although the New Testament teaches that it was because of envy that the Jews turned Jesus over to Pilate (Matt. 27:18), they deluded themselves into thinking they were doing a service to God.[8] These men weren't blasé about sin. They were so concerned about it that they refused to enter Pilate's Praetorium so that they might not be "defiled" during the Passover (John 18:28). All the while they were committing

---

8. Jesus spoke of this in John 16:2.

the most heinous sin of all time: arranging for the death of the Son of God.

The Pharisees weren't idolaters . . . at least not outwardly. But they idolized positions of power and influence and their own meritorious self-righteousness, and because of that they sought to murder God. Of course, these men didn't actually believe; they didn't trust in God or His Christ and were still dead in their sins. But they were outwardly, rigorously religious, demonstrating that rigorous religion and outward conformity to God's law doesn't signify saving faith and can be, in fact, a serious impediment to true faith. They would have protested that they had never served idols . . . and yet, their hearts were far from God. They loved "respectful greetings" and "places of honor" more than they loved God (Luke 20:46). Their wicked hearts were particularly prone to deception[9] because they had another god—the respect of men. Loving anything, even adherence to outward codes of religious behavior, more than God is idolatry, and idolatry always produces a deceived heart.[10]

Paul, a true believer, experienced heart trouble too. In Romans 7 he declared that he "joyfully concur[red] with the law of God in the inner man" (v. 22), but he saw that there was within him another force. This force waged war against the truth he had

---

9. Isaiah's scathing description of the idolater includes this portrayal: "He feeds on ashes; a deceived heart has turned him aside. And he cannot deliver himself, nor say, 'Is there not a lie in my right hand?'" (Isa. 44:20).

10. As believers, our trust must rest solely on God's love and His ability to guide and direct our hearts away from idolatry and deception. We can always trust that God will guide our hearts to perform His will, for even though the Pharisees thought that the crucifixion was their plan, it was God's:

"For truly in this city there were gathered together against Your holy servant Jesus, whom You anointed, both Herod and Pontius Pilate, along with the Gentiles and the peoples of Israel, to do whatever Your hand and Your purpose predestined to occur." (Acts 4:27–28)

The Pharisees were completely responsible for freely following their heart's wicked thoughts and desires, but even in this God ruled sovereignly. It's in that sovereign rule that we can find peace as we submit ourselves to Him.

embraced with his heart. He anguished over his false desires. On the one hand he sought after God; on the other he went after sin. On the one hand he knew that God had graciously given him all he needed; on the other hand he coveted things God had withheld from him (Rom. 7:7–8). Paul struggled because, like us, he was simultaneously sinner and justified. Like us, his heart continually whispered to him about sin's goodness and the joys to be found in disobedience, while his faith countered that all happiness was found in Christ alone. In great distress he cried out, "Wretched man that I am! Who will set me free from the body of this death?" and his answer was, "Thanks be to God through Jesus Christ our Lord!" (Rom. 7:24–25).

The God Who Knows the Real You

"Well," you might be thinking, "if my heart is so deceitful, why should I bother struggling against idolatry at all?" The answer might seem simplistic, but we should struggle against our sinful hearts because God commands us to. How will we grow in our love for the Lord with all our hearts, souls, and minds if we don't combat the ways that we fail to do so? How can we grow in our gratitude for grace if we don't see the ways in which we fail to embrace it?

This struggle against the sin in our hearts is precious because by it we learn what a great price the Lord Jesus has paid, and we will learn to be grateful for His perfect obedience in our place. It is in this struggle that we will learn to trust Him and to distrust ourselves, to hate sin and to love holiness, to cultivate humility and to long for heaven. And in the midst of it all, we'll learn the joy of increasing gratitude and the happiness that is found only in loving God.

Take refuge in the truth that your heavenly Father completely understands your heart. Even though your heart might deceive you, your heart isn't hidden to Him.

For God sees not as man sees, for . . . the LORD looks at the heart. (1 Sam. 16:7)

For the LORD searches all hearts, and understands every intent of the thoughts. (1 Chron. 28:9; see also 2 Chron. 6:30)

He knows the secrets of the heart. (Ps. 44:21; see also 139:2)

I, the LORD, search the heart, I test the mind. (Jer. 17:10)

But Jesus . . . knew what was in man. (John 2:24–25)

You, Lord . . . know the hearts of all men. (Acts 1:24)

And all the churches will know that I am He who searches the minds and hearts. (Rev. 2:23)

He knows you. He knows how you long to love Him, how you want to live for Him. He also knows where you're deceived. He knows when you're trying to kid Him into thinking that you're okay. He knows all the times when you do good works to impress others and build your own self-righteousness. He knows all the ways you use punctilious law keeping as a way to assure your heart, save yourself, and avoid the humiliation of the cross. He knows all about the ways you trust in your own goodness and look down on others. He knows about your unbelief and the ways that you seek to assure yourself by looking at your own record. He knows you through and through. That's why Jesus told His disciples, "I am the good shepherd, and I know My own" (John 10:14). Yes, He knows us completely . . . but that's not all. He also loves us utterly. Amazing grace!

The Word Diagnoses
Your Heart's Condition

Although our hearts are unknowable without His aid, God has given us a tool to use as we seek to develop wholehearted worship: the Word of God.

> For the word of God is living and powerful, and sharper than any two-edged sword, piercing even to the division of soul and spirit, and of joints and marrow, and is a discerner of the thoughts and intents of the heart. (Heb. 4:12 NKJV)

The Word of God discerns even the most hidden thoughts and designs of the heart. Only the Holy Spirit, as He works in union with His Word, can reveal our thoughts and intentions. As we read, meditate on, study, and hear preaching of the Word, we're able to get a glimpse of our inner self. As I've studied, I've been enlightened about my true thoughts, desires, and choices. "Wow!" I've thought. "That's me!" No ordinary book, trained therapist, or close friend can do this for you. Nothing can illumine your understanding to who you are except the Word of God.[11] God has given you the Word so that you can grow in your knowledge of yourself and develop true worship of Him.[12]

You and I will always struggle with knowing our heart. The more we give ourselves to know, believe, and obey the Word, the

---

11. That's why I take the time to write out verses for you.

12. Self-knowledge is the first step toward the knowledge of God. We must see "our own ignorance, vanity, poverty, infirmity, and—what is more—depravity and corruption," before we can "recognize that the true light of wisdom, sound virtue, full abundance or every good, and purity of righteousness rest in the Lord alone. To this extent we are prompted by our own ills to contemplate the good things of God; and we cannot seriously aspire to Him before we begin to become displeased with ourselves." John Calvin, *Institutes of the Christian Religion*, ed. John T. McNeill, 2 vols., Library of Christian Classics (Philadelphia: Westminster, 1960), 1:36–37.

more self-understanding we'll have, but we'll never see ourselves or God perfectly. "For now we see in a mirror dimly, but then face to face; now I know in part, but then I will know fully just as I also have been fully known" (1 Cor. 13:12). We don't need to worry about this lack of knowledge, though. We are not saved or loved because we've come to know ourselves. We are saved and loved by faith in the God who knows us completely. Of course, there will come a day when we'll know ourselves because we see Him in all His beauty, but until then we'll have to be content with clouded, dim images and pray for hearts that are willing, though incapacitated. We can trust that the Lord will illumine to us all that we need to know about our hearts when we need to know it, and we can pray with Bernard in the meantime, "Draw me, however unwilling, to make me willing; draw me, slow-footed, to make me run."[13]

The heart, as it's defined in Scripture, is amazingly complex. It's much more than Valentine cards and lace doilies. It's the wellspring of everything that you are—your aspirations, your desires, your loves. And although it is barely known by you (even with the Spirit's illumination), it's completely understood by God. By faith, we can believe that though our knowledge is always skewed and finite, we are His by grace alone. He knows us completely and yet loves us fully. Amazing grace!

The Scarlet Thread

We don't know exactly when or how the Lord worked in Rahab's heart, but it is obvious that He had, for when the spies told her to tie a cord of scarlet thread in the window for her safety, she

---

13. Bernard, *Sermons on the Song of Songs*, quoted in Calvin, *Institutes*, 1:307.

complied. Is it possible that the spies were remembering the saving blood that had been applied to the lintel and side posts of their parents' homes in Egypt? Just as the blood protected the Israelites from destruction, this red cord would preserve her from the coming judgment.

As you struggle with competing loves, you can remember the scarlet thread of Christ's blood applied to your heart. There will be times of war as you wrestle with your unbelief and idolatry, but you needn't worry about your ultimate safety. God has promised that He will complete His work in you and deliver you safely to His eternal kingdom.

> Let it be a scarlet line that you tie in the window . . . namely, an avowal of true faith in his precious blood. . . . It is a high privilege to dwell peaceably and quietly in the finished work of Christ, and in the sure immutable promise of God, who cannot lie. Why fret ye yourselves . . . and go about with a thousand anxieties when salvation's work was finished on the accursed tree, and Christ has gone into the glory, and has carried on his perfect work before his Father's face?[14]

So you see, in the same way God informed, enlightened, and conquered Rahab's heart, He can inform, enlighten, and conquer yours. He can bring to you the immeasurable peace and joy that flows out to all the world from the sacred blood that was shed upon that terrifying and glorious tree.

---

14. "A Scarlet Line in the Window, Joshua 2:21," a sermon by C. H. Spurgeon at the Metropolitan Tabernacle, from *Spurgeon's Sermons* (electronic database; Seattle: Biblesoft, 1997).

1. How does the story of Rahab encourage you?

2. What does the story of Moses prove about God's ability to work in our hearts?

3. From your studies, how would you define the heart? How has your perception of it changed?

4. Jeremiah taught that the heart was "deceitful" and "wicked." What does that mean?

5. Can you think of a specific time when you were convinced that a certain course of action was right only to find out later that you were mistaken? How can something like that happen?

6. What does the truth that God is the Heart Knower mean to you? How does it comfort you?

7

Thinking about Your God

Serve Him with a whole heart and a willing mind;
for the LORD searches all hearts, and understands
every intent of the thoughts. (1 Chronicles 28:9)

Hundreds of years before his birth, the righteous reign of young King Josiah had been foretold.[1] Although he was only eight years old when he began to rule in Judah, he was one of his nation's greatest reformers. Even though he had grown up in a nation devoted to idolatry, including even the sacrifice of children, the Lord had given Josiah a love for Him and a desire to worship Him. But Josiah was uninformed about God's law and the greatness of the sin that the people were committing. During the cleaning of the temple, the book of the law was found. King Josiah responded emotionally when it was read to him: "When the king heard the words of the book of the law, he tore his clothes" (2 Kings 22:11).

Imagine the alarm that filled the young king's heart as he heard, probably for the first time, the Word of God. That day he came face to face with God's holy law, and he abhorred himself and the sin of his people. He commanded, "Go, inquire of the LORD for me and the people and all Judah concerning the words of this

1. "He cried against the altar by the word of the LORD, and said, 'O altar, altar, thus says the LORD, "Behold, a son shall be born to the house of David, Josiah by name; and on you he shall sacrifice the priests of the high places who burn incense on you, and human bones shall be burned on you"'" (1 Kings 13:2).

book that has been found, for great is the wrath of the LORD that burns against us, because our fathers have not listened to the words of this book, to do according to all that is written concerning us" (2 Kings 22:13).

Josiah's heart was smitten. The law's work of crushing his self-confidence had been accomplished. He understood God's just wrath was burning against him and his people, and he was justifiably terrified. Josiah had an encounter with the God of the Bible that day—an encounter that changed him and his nation. The Holy Spirit caused him to comprehend the words of the law, his affections were awakened and alarmed, and his will was moved to action. He knew he needed God's mercy in a way he had never known before.

The Holy Spirit moved powerfully upon Josiah's understanding. He illumined his mind to the great sin of idolatry and the extreme danger that his nation was in. He granted him repentance, faith to believe that God would help him, and the desire to reform his nation. God's work in Josiah was effective. God enlightened his mind so that he would become the man that He had foretold he would be. As we continue to look at idolatry, remember that God can do the same thing for you: He can help you identify and crush the idols in your heart, grant you faith to believe that He will continue to be gracious to you, and enable you to find your happiness in Him.

God's Grace in Our Minds

Since it is the function of the mind to inform the affections about the love of God and to train the will to choose the right, it is the most important part of our heart. Remember your mind includes your thoughts, beliefs, understanding, memories, judgments, discernment, and conscience. Your mind is to act as a guard against ignorance, error, and unbelief. Ignorance of the will of God and error about the nature of God are two serious causes of idolatry. Josiah discovered that truth firsthand, didn't he?

If you are unaware or misinformed about God's jealous desire to be the sole focus of your worship, then you'll be more susceptible to worshiping gods of your own making. If, in error, you believe that God doesn't care about what or how you worship, you'll make your own gods and sin against Him.

Before you give in to fear or despair, remember that it's God's desire to instruct us in truth. Just as God informed Josiah, He'll also enlighten you. Remember that "there is nothing which we need to know that He is not both able and willing to acquaint us with."[2] Without His grace, we'll never understand the meaning or importance of the Word. But God hasn't deserted us or left us to try to figure things out on our own; as John 16:13 says, "The Spirit of truth . . . will guide you into all the truth" (see also Deut. 4:10; Pss. 119:73; 143:10; Matt. 11:29).

It is your Father's good pleasure to teach you about Himself, His law, and even His gracious love of lawbreakers. He does this primarily through opening your understanding to Scripture. Think back to the last time that you discovered some truth from the Bible. It's amazing how all of a sudden, out of the blue, some truth comes leaping out of the pages of Scripture, isn't it? Sometimes I think it must be the first time I've ever read it—although I know it isn't. That's the work of the Lord, enlightening your eyes and bringing you the special revelation of His truth.

In tandem with the Spirit, the Bible teaches you everything you need to know about God—who He is and how you should

2. Richard Baxter, *A Christian Directory* (Morgan, PA: Soli Deo Gloria Publications, 1996), 80.

worship Him.[3] It teaches you about His faithfulness to continue to love you and His plan to bring you into His family as a beloved son or daughter. Only as you, like Josiah, begin to see God as He is through Scripture will you begin to believe that you can put away your false gods, begin to love and trust in His mercy, and begin to worship Him in truth.

Although the Word is complete and tells us everything we need to know about God, we also need "a personal spiritual illumination by the power of the Holy Ghost."[4] The Holy Spirit must take the Scriptures He wrote and apply them to our heart, enlightening our mind, expanding our hearts to believe, and freeing us from error. By this, He enables us to war against the delusions of false worship, for we see God as He is.

Creating God in Our Image

Let's look more closely now at how our Spirit-enabled knowledge of truth can keep us from idolatry.

Idolatry is a sin that has its beginning in the mind, in our thoughts, beliefs, judgments, and imagination. God rebuked the Israelites because they had created a god in their own image: "You thought that I was just like you" (Ps. 50:21). Incorrect thinking about God's character breeds idolatry. For instance, if we imagine a more docile, controllable god or a god that can be bent by our whim, we're creating an idol. If we imagine a god who functions like a vending machine under the principle of "Christian karma," we're worshiping a false god. God is neither a doddering old grand-

---

3. John Calvin wrote, "Just as old and bleary-eyed men and those with weak vision, if you thrust before them a most beautiful volume, even if they recognize it to be some sort of writing, yet can scarcely construe two words, but with the aid of spectacles will begin to read distinctly; so Scripture, gathering up the otherwise confused knowledge of God in our minds, having dispersed our dullness, clearly shows us the true God." John Calvin, *Institutes of the Christian Religion*, ed. John T. McNeill, 2 vols., Library of Christian Classics (Philadelphia: Westminster, 1960), 1:70.

4. Ibid., 1:39.

father nor the equivalent of a celestial Santa, rewarding nice kids with goodies and punishing the naughty with lumps of coal. If we imagine that God is a demanding taskmaster who commands us to do what we cannot do and who enjoys punishing us, we've created a false god. We need to learn that God is both uncompromisingly holy and shockingly merciful . . . at the same time.

We must be careful to worship God as He has presented Himself in Scripture. He has clearly shown Himself as the one true God (Deut. 6:4), infinitely perfect and pure (Matt. 5:48), invisible (1 Tim. 1:17), not having a body (John 4:24), unchangeable (James 1:17), immense (1 Kings 8:27), eternal (Ps. 90:2), incomprehensible (Ps. 145:3), almighty (Rev. 4:8), wise (Rom. 16:27), holy (Isa. 6:3), free (Ps. 115:3), working everything according to His will and for His glory (Eph. 1:11; Rom. 11:36). He is loving (1 John 4:8), gracious, merciful, longsuffering, abundant in lovingkindness and truth. He forgives iniquity (Ex. 34:6–7) and rewards those who diligently seek Him (Heb. 11:6). He is just in all His judgments (Ps. 37:28), hates all sin (Ps. 5:5–6), and will by no means clear the guilty (Nah. 1:2–3).[5] Although this list is not exhaustive, it helps us to begin to get a glimpse of who He is. He's not like us, is He? If we worship a god who is anything less than this, or other than this, we're not worshiping the God of the Bible. We're worshiping a god of our creation.

The Foolishness of Idolatry

Not only is idolatry sinful; it is also absurd. The Old Testament speaks scathingly of the stupidity and irrationality of idolatry.[6] Reflect again on the foolishness of Rachel, who worshiped a god that could be stolen. Why would she put her trust in something

---

5. Westminster Confession of Faith, chapter 2, *Of God and the Holy Trinity*.
6. "All mankind is stupid, devoid of knowledge; every goldsmith is put to shame by his idols, for his molten images are deceitful, and there is no breath in them" (Jer. 51:17).

that was so weak it could be stolen? That really is foolish, isn't it? Your mind should guard you against this stupidity, as Isaiah said:

> Those who fashion a graven image are all of them futile. . . . Another shapes wood, he extends a measuring line; he outlines it with red chalk. He works it with planes and outlines it with a compass, and makes it like the form of a man, like the beauty of man, so that it may sit in a house.
>
> Surely he cuts cedars for himself. . . . He plants a fir, and the rain makes it grow.
>
> Then it becomes something for a man to burn, so he takes one . . . and warms himself; he also makes a fire to bake bread. He also makes a god and worships it; he makes it a graven image and falls down before it.
>
> Half of it he burns in the fire; over this half he eats meat as he roasts a roast and is satisfied. He also warms himself and says, "Aha! I am warm, I have seen the fire."
>
> But the rest of it he makes into a god, his graven image. He falls down before it and worships; he also prays to it and says, "Deliver me, for you are my god."
>
> They do not know, nor do they understand, for He has smeared over their eyes so that they cannot see and their hearts so that they cannot comprehend.
>
> No one recalls, nor is there knowledge or understanding to say, "I have burned half of it in the fire and also have baked bread over its coals. I roast meat and eat it. Then I make the rest of it into an abomination, I fall down before a block of wood!"
>
> He feeds on ashes; a deceived heart has turned him aside. And he cannot deliver himself, nor say, "Is there not a lie in my right hand?" (Isa. 44:9, 13–20)

Isaiah does a powerful job illustrating the insanity of worshiping a block of wood, doesn't he? Over one part of the wood the idolater cooks his dinner; with another part he fashions a god that he trusts will save and bless him. The idolater's mind is deceived. He doesn't comprehend or understand the absurdity of his actions. The idolater creates gods that suit him, and he irrationally trusts that they will bring him happiness. His mind is not functioning as a guard against error, is it? He's longing to create a god in his own strength; he's trying to save himself without having to believe in the Word of the Savior.

"Well," you might be thinking, "of course that's ridiculous! Anyone can see that worshiping a visible image like that is foolish—but what does that have to do with me? I wouldn't bow down before any block of wood!" Yes, thankfully, that's probably true. But think deeply here so you don't miss the significance of the Bible's warnings about idolatry. The truth is that before it was shaped into an idol, it was first crafted in the human understanding—in the imagination of the idolater. "The fact that those idols are subsequently given form in an image of wood or stone is secondary. The spirit of man begets the idolatrous image; his hand gives it birth."[7] So idols do exist on every street corner—only you can't always see them as easily as I did in Asia. We can't see them because they exist in our thoughts.

We may have grown more sophisticated in our idolatry, but we're still just as deluded, aren't we? We would never consider anything so stupid as worshiping a rock or tree—but we frequently fall into the sin of worshiping a god of our imagination . . . a god who thinks just like us, whom we can command and manipulate for

---

7. J. Douma, *The Ten Commandments: Manual for the Christian Life* (Phillipsburg, NJ: P&R, 1996), 69.

our pleasure,[8] to serve our ambitions.[9] We want to find a way to save ourselves, to satisfy our own hearts, to prove our okay-ness to ourselves and others. And we really don't want any outside help to do so. "I've got this . . ." is the mantra of the idolater.

It is because we have such a bent to create gods who are more to our liking that our minds must continually be informed and corrected. Like Josiah, we need concentrated doses of truth on a daily basis about the God who really is.

"We ought not to think," Paul preached, "that the Divine Nature is . . . an image formed by the art and thought of man" (Acts 17:29). No, Paul teaches—God is not formed by our thought. In fact, the opposite is true—we are formed by His thought! We must learn to put away the gods of our imagination: gods that promise happiness in exchange for our worship. Just as in the case of King Josiah, that can happen only as the Spirit uses the Word to bring us into the blazing light of His person.

Naming Your Gods

"Well," you might be wondering, "how would I recognize a god in my imagination? How could I identify it?" This is where our discussion about happiness will help.

Where Is Your Happiness?

To identify your idols, begin to look at the thoughts and imaginations that promise you happiness. Ancient cultures had gods for all the misunderstood forces of nature, including gods of fertility and harvest. They worshiped these gods because children and good crops were recognized as sources of happiness. They were willing

---

8. Calvin writes, "Man's mind, full as it is of pride and boldness, dares to imagine a god according to its own capacity; as it sluggishly plods, indeed is overwhelmed with the crassest ignorance, it conceives an unreality and an empty appearance as God." Calvin, *Institutes*, 1:108.

9. Ibid., 1:70.

to sacrifice a portion of their harvest or even a child if they could control their environment and gain some assurance of future joys. They trusted in false gods because they believed there was some profit in it, and we do the same thing. It was in light of this that Jeremiah prophesied:

> For the customs of the peoples are delusion;
> Because it is wood cut from the forest,
> The work of the hands of a craftsman with a cutting tool.
> They decorate it with silver and with gold;
> They fasten it with nails and with hammers
> So that it will not totter.
> Like a scarecrow in a cucumber field are they,
> And they cannot speak;
> They must be carried,
> Because they cannot walk!
> Do not fear them,
> For they can do no harm,
> Nor can they do any good. (Jer. 10:3–5)

Jeremiah illustrates the foolishness of trusting in a god that has to be hammered up so that it won't fall over. He compares it to a scarecrow that frightens stupid birds. Rational people aren't afraid of scarecrows because they know that a scarecrow can't harm them. They don't worship them because they know that scarecrows have no power. But people trust in idols because they believe there is some benefit in doing so, and they are afraid of what might happen if they don't.[10]

---

10. This is the attitude that is seen in the Israelites after they had fled to Egypt. They believed that their idols would bring them blessing and that turning from them was a curse:
"Then all the men who were aware that their wives were burning sacrifices to other gods, along with all the women who were standing by, as a large assembly, including all the people who were living in Pathros in the land of Egypt, responded to Jeremiah, saying,

There is no profit to be gained from worshiping false gods, but people do so because they're deceived. They might be deceived about the blessedness of worshiping the true God. They might be afraid of what might happen if they trusted only in God. Just remember that whenever we worship idols we do so because we're convinced that it will bring us happiness. We believe that there will be some benefit from it. And then, when it seems that things aren't working out the way we want, we try harder and harder to find satisfaction but always come up empty.

Serving false gods is irrational—the mind is believing in and trusting a falsehood, and the affections and will follow along. We know it doesn't make sense to bow down before anything other than the Creator God. Only He can bring happiness and joy. Only He can satisfy us, but we hate to give up our little gods. Let's take time now to consider our thoughts and beliefs more closely to see if we can find any false gods lurking there.

Gods of Our Thoughts

Instead of fashioning idols out of wood or stone, we fashion them in our imagination—worshiping that which we believe will bring us happiness. We don't carve a good spouse out of a piece of pine, but we worship the thought of the joy that one would bring us. We don't chisel out a facsimile of the self-sufficient man or woman, but we believe that's where our joy can be found. We believe that our

---

'As for the message that you have spoken to us in the name of the LORD, we are not going to listen to you! But rather we will certainly carry out every word that has proceeded from our mouths, by burning sacrifices to the queen of heaven and pouring out drink offerings to her, just as we ourselves, our forefathers, our kings and our princes did in the cities of Judah and in the streets of Jerusalem; for then we had plenty of food and were well off and saw no misfortune. But since we stopped burning sacrifices to the queen of heaven and pouring out drink offerings to her, we have lacked everything and have met our end by the sword and by famine.'" (Jer. 44:15–18)

Hab. 2:18 reiterates the same thought: "What profit is the idol when its maker has carved it, or an image, a teacher of falsehood?"

happiness is bound up in having our expectation fulfilled. These beliefs function as gods just as surely as if we had carved them from wood or overlaid them with silver. Our thoughts and dreams of imaginary happiness are valuable to us. We can't envision life without them.

Our beliefs about the sources of joy (a spouse or success, for instance) are frequently experienced as colorful imaginations that captivate our heart. Paul told the Corinthians to "[cast] down imaginations, and . . . [bring] into captivity every thought to the obedience of Christ" (2 Cor. 10:5 KJV). In order to "flee from idolatry" (1 Cor. 10:14), we must be vigilant to judge our every thought and imagination by the Word. We must analyze whether they are truly good. Then, if so, we must ask whether our passion for them has overshadowed our passion for God. Whether they are godly thoughts that we have elevated to an improper place of prominence in our hearts (the belief that a spouse could bring us greater joy than God) or whether they are ungodly delusions (the imagination of how happy we would be if we were rich), they can function as a god. In short, we must discern whether we're believing the truth or a lie. As you can see, idols live in our thoughts, beliefs, and imaginations, and it's there that they must be annihilated.

The lies that we commonly believe—lies that are peddled by Satan and the world—cloud our thinking about God's true nature and the source of happiness. The lie that happiness can be found in something other than God is the deception from which all our idolatry flows. What might some of these lies look like? Let me give you some examples and see if they resonate with you.

- In order to be truly happy, I must have a spouse who is godly, romantic, responsible, and a good communicator.
- In order to be truly happy, I must have obedient children who make me look good.

- In order to be truly happy, I must have a good job where I am respected and well paid so that I don't have to rely on anyone else.
- In order to be truly happy, I must be loved and appreciated by others.
- In order to be happy, I need the approval of others and/or myself.
- In order to be truly happy, I must feel safe from all calamities.
- In order to be truly happy, I must be able to look at my life and see how I'm growing, how I'm progressing, how I'm getting better and better everyday.

It is the role of your mind, as it has been enlightened by the Spirit and Scripture, to correct your thinking when you believe lies and begin to worship thoughts of imagined happiness. Although this list is not exhaustive, it serves to demonstrate how easy it is for us to be deceived. Unless the mind is acting as a watchman, you'll fall into error. You'll begin to believe the lie that a good spouse or child or job or any created thing is the source of happiness. And then, just as soon as you do that, you'll be worshiping a false god. Remember, any time your worship is focused on anything other than God, that's idolatry.

Let me try to illustrate this further. If you believe that you can be happy only if you're well respected on the job, then all your efforts will be focused on gaining your employer's approval. You'll be angry when you aren't getting the affirmation you long for; you'll look for ways to make yourself appear better than your peers; you'll live for the perceived happiness of your employer saying, "I appreciate you." There's nothing wrong with trying to be a good employee, for the Lord's sake, as one facet of your worship (Col. 3:22–24). But if you're doing so because you love the false god

"My Employer's Approval" or "I Must Be a Success," you're breaking the first commandment—and you've been deceived.

False Gods Breed Disobedience

The struggle with idolatry and deception began with Eve and continues to this day. Eve was deceived into thinking that happiness could be found in disobedience to God. Every time we sin, it's because we're deceived too. We foolishly think that happiness is to be found in pursuing the lies that whisper seductively in our heart. We sin because we believe that there's some happiness to be gained by it. It's then that our thoughts about happiness become our god. I'm not saying that we're not fully responsible for our sin because we're deceived. We are completely culpable for all our sin because we don't believe God's Word and we trust in gods of our own imagination. It's idolatrous to make our imaginations more important than joyful obedience to the Lord. Remember, our idols always come to us dressed as goodness.

Our idolatrous beliefs become evident as we find ourselves habitually sinning in some particular way. If I discover, for instance, that I frequently respond in anger when criticized, then I need to consider what idolatrous thought or imagination is at the root of my anger. To do this, I should ask myself the following questions:

- What do I believe about the source of true happiness in this circumstance?
- What do I believe about God in this circumstance?
- What do I believe about myself—my rights, my goals, my desires?
- What am I trusting in to make me happy?
- Why is this person's opinion so important to me? Do I believe in justification by man's approval?

For instance, in this case, I might answer:

- *What do I believe about the source of true happiness in this circumstance?* I'm believing that happiness can be found only when others respect me. My belief, "I Must Be Respected," has become my god, and it produces bitter fruit for anyone who dares to challenge me.
- *What do I believe about God in this circumstance?* I'm doubting His character. I believe that He's not good. I believe that if He were good He would protect me from attack. My desire (I shouldn't be criticized) colors my appraisal of Him and causes me to seek to remake Him into my image. "Why, if He were really good," I think, "He would make others treat me the way I want to be treated!" Instead of thinking that God isn't good, perhaps the truth is that He isn't powerful. *If God were powerful, He could control how others treat me.* (Do you see how important it is to have a biblical understanding of God's character?)
- *What do I believe about myself—my rights, my goals, my desires?* I believe I have a right to be respected on the job. I think I should never be criticized. Whenever I am criticized, I view myself as a victim of others' wrongdoing. I believe happiness will continue to elude me if people disapprove of me. I ignore the truth that it doesn't matter who approves of me or even if I approve of myself (2 Cor. 10:18). I believe that it is more important to have others' approval than God's. Could this be because others are my god?
- *What am I trusting in?* Instead of trusting in God—that He has allowed this difficulty into my life for my good (and ultimate happiness)—I'm trusting that people have

the power to make me happy. I have tied their approval of me to my worth. I need to see my circumstance as God's gift to open my eyes to my idolatry and free me from it. Instead of getting sinfully angry when I'm criticized, I need to rejoice in God's faithful discipline (Prov. 25:12).

- *What justifies me?* In this case I'm thinking that the opinion of others justifies or makes me okay; I'm believing that I need the welcome and approval of others and forgetting that I already have the complete welcome and approval of my Heavenly Father because of my faith in Christ's perfect obedience and substitutionary death.

- *Who saves me?* In this case I'm thinking I have to save myself. I'm assuming that the approval of other people means something ultimate about my worth, my "save-ability," my "love-ability." Of course, the truth is that I don't deserve nor can I earn God's salvation. It is given to me by grace through faith in Jesus alone. I don't deserve it. I can't earn it. My record has nothing to do with it.

Are there circumstances in which you find yourself sinning habitually? If so, ask yourself these questions and you're liable to find sinful thoughts and imaginations at the heart of the problem. This will help you to see the reasons behind it so you can begin to address the source. Instead of just trying to control my temper when I'm criticized, for instance, I need to understand that the reason I'm angry is because I crave and worship other people's opinions of me, and I'm seeking to justify myself. I need to repent of my thoughts about myself and agree with God that only He is worthy of praise (at the same time that I repent of my sinful anger).

If I believe the lies of the world, the flesh, and the Devil, then they become the biggest concerns in my life. My mind entertains thoughts of how happy I would be if everyone approved of me, if I knew I really were worthy of love. When these thoughts captivate me, the worship of God becomes subsidiary. My imaginations take center stage, and God becomes a mere stagehand whose purpose is to make me look good. My thoughts have become my god, and I'm willing to do anything—even sin—to get what I believe will make me happy.

Your Mind's Business

Your mind is to guard you from idolatry. It should filter and judge every thought, especially those colored by imagination. Remember that Paul told the Corinthians to "[cast] down imaginations, and every high thing that exalteth itself against the knowledge of God, and . . . [bring] into captivity every thought to the obedience of Christ" (2 Cor. 10:5 KJV). Your mind, particularly your conscience, should examine every thought and cast down those that are raised in opposition to the true knowledge of God and His saving love. Because He has loved and welcomed you, you no longer need to seek love and welcome from others. Every thought must be brought into obedience to the gospel. Just as Josiah crushed the idols in his day, by faith you can begin to root out and crush your idolatrous imaginations and everything that tells you that you need more than He's given you in Christ. You can't accomplish this in your own strength, but by the power of the Spirit you can grow in your single-minded worship of the living God and destroy your false gods.

FOR FURTHER THOUGHT

1. Why is it important for you to have a correct understanding of God?

2. How does God inform you about His nature? What particular characteristic of His do you especially rejoice in? Find verses that illustrate this truth.

3. How would you explain the role of idolatry in modern man to a sixth grader?

4. Identify any areas where you have expectations that function as gods. Think about your imaginations during the day. How do you see yourself?

5. Track your habitual sin to discover areas of idolatry, using the questions on page 131.

6. Can you see any ways in which you are seeking to justify yourself? What are they? What is the answer to the struggle for self-justification?

7. Write out a prayer that God, by the Holy Spirit, will illumine your heart and make you aware of your idols. When He does so, don't give up in self-loathing or despair; repent and ask Him to teach you the truth about His nature. Plead with Him to give you a heart that would love and worship only Him.

8

Longing for God

Besides You, I desire nothing on earth.
(Psalm 73:25)

Like Rachel before her, Hannah longed for a child. Although her husband, Elkanah, loved her, Peninnah, his other wife, "would provoke her bitterly to irritate her, because the LORD had closed her womb" (1 Sam. 1:6). We can imagine the cruel remarks and smirking looks that were directed toward Hannah when Elkanah played with Peninnah's children. What torment Hannah must have known!

When the family took their annual trip to Shiloh to worship God, Hannah was so overwhelmed with grief at her childlessness that she refused to eat. But in God's grace, she went to the temple, and "prayed to the LORD and wept bitterly" (1 Sam. 1:10). Unlike Rachel before her, we have no record that she angrily demanded a child. Her desire was centered on the Lord, so she poured out her heart before Him.

As she wrestled in silent prayer, God's grace rearranged her desires. She was assured that He remembered her. She willingly vowed to give the desire of her heart to Him. She prayed, "O LORD of hosts, if You will indeed look on the affliction of Your maidservant and remember me, and . . . give Your maidservant a son, then I will give him to the LORD all the days of his life" (1 Sam. 1:11). She walked away from that humbling prayer a changed woman.

She found the true source of joy, the true source of her justification, and her face reflected it (1 Sam. 1:18).

Hannah had a strong desire. She longed for a son to love and nurture for the Lord. But Hannah's desire was not her god. She didn't want a child merely to put an end to Peninnah's cruelty. She wanted a child she could rear to glorify and serve her God.

Hannah's worship of God is seen in the name she gave her son. Remember how Rachel named her son Joseph, showing her discontented desire for more? Hannah named her son Samuel, meaning, "I have asked him of the LORD" (1 Sam. 1:20). She knew her son was a gift from God. Every time she spoke his name she remembered he was an answer to prayer. He belonged to God. God graciously gratified Hannah because she had made her request in faith.[1]

The Gift of Our Affections

In this chapter, we're going to look at our affections. Remember, affections are our longings, desires, and feelings.[2] Our longings and desires are crucial to the study of idolatry because they prompt and channel worship. They are the driving force behind everything we do.

Think again about Hannah's strong desire to have a child for the Lord. What did it motivate her to do? She prayed and poured out her soul before Him. It drove her to deep, heartfelt worship. Just like Hannah, you and I have deep desires and longings. We embrace treasures in our hearts. We long for that one something that will bring us ultimate happiness.

---

1. That's not the end of Hannah's story. The Bible tells us she had five more children after Samuel. God abundantly satisfied her desire—He not only gave her the son she prayed for (and ultimately gave up) but also other sons and daughters. What a gracious God we serve!

2. We are going to look at our emotions in following chapters, but since our thoughts and desires give birth to our emotions, it's better to focus on the cause (thoughts, desires) rather than the effect (emotions).

The Nature of Desire

That we all have desires is a given. There are, however, two questions that we must wrestle with: (1) What is the source of our desire? (2) How can we judge whether our desires are idolatrous or God-centered?

The Lust in Our Hearts

The Bible speaks at great length about desires. It frequently uses the word *lust* when doing so. We usually use this word in reference to strong sexual desire, but the Bible uses it more broadly. Consider the following verses:

> But each one is tempted when he is carried away and enticed by his own lust. (James 1:14)

> You lust and do not have. . . . You are envious and cannot obtain. . . . You ask with wrong motives, so that you may spend it on your pleasures. (James 4:2–3)[3]

> For all that is in the world, the lust of the flesh and the lust of the eyes and the boastful pride of life, is not from the Father. . . . The world is passing away, and also its lusts. (1 John 2:16–17)

In these verses (and many others)[4] the word translated "lust," "long for," "desire," or "pleasure" is *epithumia*, which means a longing, craving, or strong desire. It has positive uses, such as in our

---

3. The word translated here as "pleasures" is the Greek *hedone*, which means "to please" in the sense of sensual delight and, by implication, desire (Strong's Exhaustive Concordance).

4. See also Luke 22:15; John 8:44; Rom. 1:24; 7:7–8; Gal. 5:16, 24; Phil. 1:23; Col. 3:5; 1 Thess. 2:17; 4:5; 1 Tim. 6:9; 2 Tim. 2:22; 3:6; 4:3; Titus 2:12; 3:3; James 1:14–15; 1 Peter 1:14; 2:11; 4:2–3; 2 Peter 1:4; 2:10, 18; 3:3; 1 John 2:16–17; Jude 16, 18.

Lord's statement, "I have earnestly desired to eat this Passover with you" (Luke 22:15).[5] Usually, however, it has a negative connotation. The New Testament writers saw desires, lusts, cravings, and longings as motivating factors in sinful behavior.[6] Although a desire may not be sinful per se, it may give rise to sin if it's too highly cherished.

For instance, to desire a spouse is not sinful.[7] If, however, a woman sins while trying to obtain a spouse or because she resents not having one, then what could be a holy desire has become an evil one. It has become evil because she has switched loyalties from a ruling love and desire for God to the love and desire for a husband. She's made a god of what should be a good desire by loving and serving it before God. She has turned it into an evil—an idol.

You see this principle in the lives of Rachel and Hannah. Rachel's desire for children was sinful because it had taken God's place in her heart. Hannah's desire wasn't sinful, because it wasn't her god. Although she suffered terribly in her barrenness, she desired a son to enhance her worship and enjoyment of Him; she humbly bowed before His will. Your desires may not be morally wrong in themselves, but the place of prominence they occupy in your heart may make them so.

Of course, there are desires that are always sinful. For instance, to desire another man's wife is always sinful. Unlike godly desires, the prominence of this desire doesn't make the desire evil. This desire is wicked in itself. It is sinful even if it is never acted upon. One

---

5. Paul also had "the desire to depart and be with Christ" (Phil. 1:23) and had a "great desire" to see the Thessalonians (1 Thess. 2:17).

6. In Gal. 5:16 Paul says, "Walk by the Spirit, and you will not carry out the desire of the flesh." He shows how the desires of the flesh give birth to the deeds of the flesh: "immorality, impurity, sensuality, idolatry, sorcery, enmities, strife, jealousy, outbursts of anger, disputes, dissensions, factions, envying, drunkenness, carousing, and things like these" (Gal. 5:19–21). See also James 1:14–16, "But each one is tempted when he is carried away and enticed by his own lust."

7. "He who finds a wife finds a good thing and obtains favor from the LORD" (Prov. 18:22).

who has this desire has sinned against God because he's desiring what God has forbidden.[8]

All people have desires, longings, and lusts. Only Christians, however, have the capacity for holy desires.[9] Believers and unbelievers have lusts and desires that drive them to act in certain ways. Why is this? Is this part of how we were created?

Created to Desire God

If you're perplexed about the true nature of desires, you're not alone. There seems to be a lot of confusion about the source and nature of desires, longings, and "needs." We must be careful to define the origin and quality of our desires the way the Bible does. In order to do so, let's first consider God's design of Adam.

God lovingly created Adam and Eve to function in certain ways. The design of Adam's body (his outer man) was a direct reflection of God's chosen place for mankind in the world. For instance, Adam didn't have gills because he had been created to live on land, in a garden, rather than a pond. Adam's body enabled him to fit perfectly into his niche in creation. God gave our parents everything they needed to live in their environment.

Not only did God create Adam and Eve's bodies to fulfill a specific role; He also created them with certain mental and spiritual capacities that defined their role in creation. He gave them a heart—an inner person with a mind, affections, and will. He made them thinking, desiring, feeling, and choosing beings. They were

---

8. See Matt. 5:22 and 28, where Jesus teaches about the sinfulness of desires that merely reside in our hearts even though they haven't been acted upon.

9. Rom. 3:10–29; Eph. 2:3; 5:3–5; Col. 3:5–7; Titus 3:3. The New Testament clearly teaches that those who are outside God's covenantal family are enslaved to their lusts and unable to desire anything that is not sinful. Even if an unbeliever seems to be doing something good (such as giving to the poor), the desires that motivate this behavior are not God-centered (for His glory) but man-centered (for his glory) and therefore sinful.

set apart from the rest of creation because God had "breathed into [their] nostrils the breath of life" (Gen. 2:7).

God created Adam and Eve with the capacity to experience great happiness in grateful relationship with Him and each other. He also placed within them the desire to perform specific tasks within God's created order and to enjoy doing so. They found happiness by taking their place in God's creation because they had been designed to serve and fellowship with their Creator and one another. They were perfectly fitted for the task.

Let's look closely at God's design, especially the capacities He gave mankind to fulfill its role. We'll see that mankind's desires flowed out of God's created pattern.

Created in the Likeness and Image of God

Unlike the rest of God's creation, Adam was created in the likeness and image of God. "Then God said, 'Let Us make man in Our image, according to Our likeness; and let them rule. . . .' God created man in His own image, in the image of God He created him; male and female He created them" (Gen. 1:26–27).[10]

Adam and Eve were both created as a reflection of God.[11] They were like God in some ways and unlike Him in other ways.[12]

10. See also Gen. 5:1; 9:6, Eccles. 7:29; Acts 17:26, 28–29; 1 Cor. 11:7; 2 Cor. 3:18; Eph. 4:24; Col. 3:10; James 3:9.

11. Both Adam and Eve were equally created in the image of God. Although they were equal before God, Eve was created with differing capacities and callings. Adam was created first to reflect and worship God (as was Eve), but Eve was also given a secondary calling: to honor Adam and be his helper. It is due to this difference in design that women frequently think, desire, and sin in ways that correspond to their "helper" nature.

12. As we saw in chapter 7, God is a Spirit, invisible, but Adam wasn't invisible because God had given him a physical body. Adam wasn't present everywhere; he wasn't almighty or all-knowing. He was dependent upon God for life, while God is independent and free—not needing anything. Adam existed in time, living within the confines of days, months, and seasons. The eternal God exists completely outside of time. While Adam reflected God in a way that no other part of the creation did, there are distinct ways in which God differed from Adam.

They were unlike God because although they were created in His image, they weren't God. They were part of the creation; God was the Creator. Nevertheless our first parents reflected God. They were able to think and reason. They had longings and desires; they experienced emotion. They had the capacity to work and choose according to their strongest preferences. God gave them the desire to rule over the creation and to experience joy in obeying God and fulfilling God's design. They had the capacity to enjoy relationships with God and others. He designed mankind to fit perfectly into His creation, completely dependent upon Him, holy and righteous.

Adam and Eve's Created Purpose

As the capstone of all creation, mankind was to reflect God. Here's a summary of how Adam and Eve mirrored God's nature through their roles and desires.

- Like God, Adam and Eve had the capacity and passion to rule over creation (Gen. 1:26).
- Like Him, they had the ability and longing to be fruitful by reproducing others who would image them (Gen. 1:28).
- Like God, they loved work. They had the capacity and desire to subdue nature; they cultivated the garden; they observed and delighted in the days and seasons; they grew in understanding of the world (Gen. 1:14, 28; 2:5, 15, 19).
- Like their Creator, they sought to sustain life. They used the resources of creation (Gen. 1:29); they ate from the plants and the trees and drank from the river that was in the garden.
- Like Him, they appreciated and created beauty and order (Gen. 2:9, 15, 19); Adam named and classified the animals; he and Eve observed the beauty of the trees.

- As He did, they rested from work for a time of fellowship. They walked with the Lord in the "cool of the day" (Gen. 2:3; 3:8).
- Like the Trinity, they had the capacity and desire to achieve "oneness" and unity (Gen. 2:18, 20–21, 23) while maintaining their uniqueness (Gen. 2:20–25). They had unfettered relationship and communication because they were alike in a way that was different from the rest of creation. Adam and Eve knew one another but were not sinfully self-aware. They were naked and were unashamed (Gen. 2:25).
- Like the Trinity, they enjoyed relationship and unity with others, becoming one with them in a similar, yet less intimate, way (Gen. 1:27).
- They had the ability and desire to be one with their Creator (who was like them, but different) through loving fellowship, joyful service, and wholehearted worship (Gen. 2:16–17).[13]
- Like God, they loved to rejoice in His person by reflecting Him to all creation, including the angels, and bringing Him pleasure.

As the crown of God's creation, Adam and Eve were given the capacity and desire to live a happy life, filled with worship, fellowship, and work. We can hardly imagine the glory and bliss they knew as they worked together, cultivating the garden and walking with the Lord in the cool of the day. They had been perfectly designed by God to fit into the place He had for them, and they loved it![14]

---

13. God placed restrictions upon Adam. As long as Adam and Eve obeyed God's word, they enjoyed open fellowship, service, and worship. Once they sinned, they were driven from God's presence.

14. How Eve and Adam could be tempted to sin is beyond this discussion.

The Shattered Mirror

We know that Adam and Eve's bliss ended because of disobedience. When they were deceived by Satan, sin entered. Sin brought not only physical and spiritual death but also the marring of Adam's nature. Since the fall, everyone's hearts (including their desires) have been "warped out of shape."[15] Where once they had perfect physical and mental capabilities and unsullied desires, we now have bodies that sicken and die. Our hearts (minds, affections, and will) have become desperately sick and wicked (Jer. 17:9). Instead of living in joyful union with God, reflecting Him through loving worship, fellowship, and work, every intent of fallen mankind's thoughts has become "only evil continually" (Gen. 6:5). Instead of our abilities and desires being a source of obedience and joy, they have become a snare, bringing sin and sorrow. Here lies the problem with our desires: our hearts, the founts from which all our sin flows (Matt. 12:34), have ceased to be God-centered and have become self-centered. We are curved in on ourselves in every area of our being. Rather than living life to reflect God for His glory, man lives for his own glory, seeking happiness in his own reflection. Rather than living in humble submission to God's word, trusting that His way is best, we rely on our own understanding (Prov. 3:5).

Think with me for a moment about some (certainly not all) of the ways God's initial design for Adam and Eve has been damaged and distorted by sin.

The Desire to Rule

Instead of desiring to rule over creation for God's glory, man's desire to rule has become self-focused. Men and women sinfully lord it

15. "The English word *depraved* was derived from words that mean 'crooked' or 'warped out of shape.'" Jay Adams, *More than Redemption* (Phillipsburg, NJ: P&R, 1979), 140.

over others, becoming cruel and demanding, relishing power and control. We crave respect, desiring that others think well of us, rather than seeking to respect and honor God and others who reflect Him. Wives seek to usurp authority over their husbands. Husbands either abdicate their role or demand unreasonable obedience. We fail to humbly submit to God, and we set ourselves up as monarchs.

The Desire for Physical Oneness

Instead of desiring to use our sexuality for God's glory, as a way to reflect God's unity, enhance oneness, and produce children to love God, we worship sex. We bow down before pleasure and power and disregard God-reflecting relationship, commitment, and communication. We relish self-focused relationships that don't mirror anything more than a shallow physical oneness.[16] We seek to build a kingdom of our own and use our kids' success as a way to justify ourselves, to enhance our resumes.

Working for His Own Pleasure

Instead of desiring to subdue and enhance nature through God-glorifying physical and intellectual work, we become workaholics seeking joy in the respect of others and the pleasures of riches. We crave security, comfort, and significance. We trust in our abilities and cherish self-reliance; we cheat others (who have been made in God's likeness) for profit. We become slaves to the clock. Or we may be lazy, serving gods of sleep, comfort, and freedom from responsibility. We may gamble or steal, desiring riches without work. We waste the time that God has given us, mindlessly living each day without a thought of God or eternity. We seek to justify ourselves through our own labors, rather than receiving justification as a gift of Jesus' labors.

16. Then, when children are conceived, many people kill them in the womb, just as the Israelites sacrificed their children to their idols.

Consuming the Creation

Instead of desiring to use the resources of creation for life and to reflect reliance on the God who maintains the world, we place the consumable pleasures of creation above God. Men and women may eat gluttonously or drink to excess. Instead of reflecting God through stewardship of the creation, including our bodies, people live greedily and callously ravage the natural world for pleasure.

The Desire for Beauty

Rather than desiring to enjoy the beauty and order of creation for God's glory, we deify outward appearances. We long for others to worship our beauty and creativity. We make a god of our physique, home, clothing, car, or anything that reflects our glory, beauty, or worth.

The Longing for Rest

Instead of desiring a time of restful and loving fellowship with our Creator, we use the time away from work in any of a myriad of godless activities. Our God-given desire for peaceful communion and rest on the Sabbath has been corrupted by self-focus so that rest from work is spent in shallow detachment binge-watching television or reading frivolous books, or, ultimately, in idleness in our retirement years.

The Desire for Oneness

Rather than desiring a oneness that reflects the oneness in the Trinity, we desire it to show our own worth. We worship the thought of being loved, cared for, and appreciated independent from our Creator. Instead of focusing on the joy of loving, caring for, and appreciating a spouse, we focus on our own desires. Instead of loving God and others, we fight for dominance, seeking to be worshiped and obeyed. We may despise differences we see in each other, seeking to change our spouse into our own image. Or we may fear these differences, sinfully molding ourselves into the image of our spouse. Communication becomes a tool to achieve these ends by demanding or manipulating a spouse through unkind, bitter, angry, or malicious speech. We think that we are justified by our relationships, by how much we are loved and appreciated, rather than by faith in Jesus alone.

The Desire for Friends

Instead of desiring relationship, fellowship, and unity with others to glorify God and as a means to love and serve them for Christ's sake, men and women desire friends so they can feel good about themselves—so that they feel accepted and valuable. We despise and fear the isolated person who doesn't fit in. We develop relationships in civic or political organizations, cheer with others at sporting events, and pursue entertainment or recreation, because we long to be part of a group—and the more powerful the group, the better. Since the fall, this desire to be one with others has been severely marred by a godless self-focus, just as it was at the tower of Babel.[17] Can't you hear the same cry, "Let us make a name for ourselves," resounding at every championship ball game? The sinful desire to be one with others may cause a man to squander time and money on professional sports. It may cause a woman to idle away hours on social media, trying to prove she is worthy to be loved, to be "friended."

The Chief End of Man

Finally, and most importantly, our foremost desire—to glorify God and enjoy Him by fulfilling all His will—has been marred almost beyond recognition. Since the fall, mankind's basic desire

---

17. Don't fail to miss the sinfulness of the builders' desires: "Come, let us build for ourselves a city, and a tower whose top will reach into heaven, and let us make for ourselves a name, otherwise we will be scattered abroad over the face of the whole earth" (Gen. 11:4). Note the sarcasm in God's reply, "Behold, they are one people, and they all have the same language. And this is what they began to do, and now nothing which they purpose to do will be impossible for them" (Gen. 11:6). Today, the reason we'll never be able to achieve worldwide unity (a new world order) is because God has confused our language and scattered us (Gen. 11:9).

has been to glorify and enjoy himself by doing what he thinks will make him happy. Due to sin, men and women fail to seek the one true source of happiness, God. Man will always desire to devote himself in some way to worship, relationships, and work because of God's imprint on his soul, but these desires are now thoroughly self-focused and distorted. Now, rather than worshiping his Creator and finding happiness in God, he'll create a god in his own image; rather than reflecting oneness with others for God's glory, he'll pursue relationships primarily for his glory and pleasure; rather than working so that God's works would be known and glorified by others, he chases after and loves money, respect, and prestige. Because he has been created in God's image, he still retains some vestige of God's design for him, but now his worship, relationships, and work have become self-focused and idolatrous.

Figure 8.1 is a summary of Adam's pre-fall desires contrasted with fallen man's.

God created Adam and Eve to fill distinct roles. He placed within them both the ability and the desire to fit perfectly into His world. By living out their roles, they imaged God. Since the fall, though, everything has changed. Sinful desires now rule us. Without God's direct intervention through Jesus Christ, our desires remain hopelessly damaged. No matter how we try to reform ourselves, we'll never regain the sinless abilities and desires we need to live the life for which we were created. We have been forever driven from paradise by God; an angel with a flaming sword blocks our return.

There is only one hope of regaining what's been lost, of recovering holy desires that produce God-centered worship; only one hope of restoration to fellowship with God and others; only one hope of experiencing the God-centeredness of our created nature. Our only hope is to be reborn in the image of Jesus Christ—the only Man who ever fulfilled His role in creation—and to receive from Him the righteous record of always living to please His Father.

Fig. 8.1. Adam's Pre-Fall Desires and Fallen Man's Desires

Adam's God-Given Sinless Desires Glorified God and Mirrored His Image by	Fallen Man's Idolatrous Desires Glorify Man's Own Image and Ignore God by
Ruling over creation, thereby bringing honor and respect to God and joy to himself.	Seeking control over nature and others to satisfy his craving for self-respect and honor.
Physically becoming one with his spouse to enhance unity and joy. Producing children who would love and worship God.	Using his sexuality to pursue his own pleasure and power. Using his children to glorify himself and build his own kingdom.
Subduing nature through joyful work accomplished for the pleasure of God.	Exalting his own significance, comfort, and worth by earning money and/or prestige.
Thankfully stewarding the resources of creation to sustain his and others' lives.	Greedily consuming the creation for his own pleasure and mismanaging his resources.
Enjoying the world by observing and classifying its beauty, design, and order.	Striving to beautify himself and his surroundings and ignoring God's beauty.
Happily engaging in a time of rest and fellowship with his Creator and with others, primarily on the Sabbath but also throughout all of life.	Pursuing self-focused work or time-wasting recreations instead of God-centered fellowship.
Using communication to become one with his spouse so that they, together, would complete all of God's work, find joy in their differences, and please him.	Trying to remake his spouse into his own image and using his spouse to make him feel loved, needed, and accepted. Using the gift of speech to obtain the respect he craves.
Joining with others to complete the work God has assigned them for their mutual benefit and fellowship.	Joining with others so he can overcome feelings of "alienation" and obtain power.
Glorifying and enjoying God in everything for his own good and God's pleasure.	Glorifying and enjoying himself in everything he thinks, says, and does for his own good and personal pleasure.

In order to be reborn into this new image, we must enter another garden[18]—one with a flaming sword that has been thrust into the side of the perfect God-Man as He hung upon another tree. We must eat and drink from *this* tree to know the truth that can remake our minds, affections, and wills. We throw ourselves on Christ and His mercy, confessing and repenting not only our sinful actions but also our sinful desires. We must repent of the desire to steal God's place by making other gods. By the power of the Spirit we must put to death our old desires and seek new, godly ones. It is only through faith in Christ that we, like another repentant thief, can regain access to paradise.[19]

The life and death of Jesus Christ is sufficient to free you from your old nature and slowly remake you into His image. He can do so because He perfectly fulfilled all His Father's will.

All you need to be remade into the image of God is trust in the perfection of Jesus Christ. As you abide in Him (pursuing unity and dependency) and in faith seek to follow His commands, you'll find that your desires are gradually transformed. He'll work in your heart to enable you to lay down your desires for self-worship and self-love, and He'll place within you the desire to worship and love Him. This will happen as we are assured that His perfect record is ours and we no longer need to seek to save or justify ourselves. Our desire to live in grateful obedience for His perfect life and substitutionary death will free us from the sense that we have anything left to prove about our save-ability, our okay-ness. We are loved. We are forgiven.

Our first query was, What is the source of our desires? As you can see, our desires were God's design, but they have been so marred

---

18. Is it coincidence that "in the place where He was crucified there was a garden" (John 19:41)?

19. "And He said to him, 'Truly I say to you, today you shall be with Me in Paradise'"(Luke 23:43).

by sin that now only a faint shadow remains. The second question was, How can we judge our desires? Unregenerate man's desires are always sinful and self-focused.[20] And even though believers have been given new hearts, we must not trust them because of remaining sin. You can judge your desires by asking yourself, "Does this fulfill God's design (as seen in Christ)?" Then, if it does, ask yourself, "Does Jesus Christ occupy the first place in this desire? Is He my God, or have I made a god of this longing?"[21]

Satisfied in Him

The wonderful truth is that all our longings are met in Christ. He's come to give us abundant life, but He doesn't do so by satisfying sinful desires. He satisfies us by turning our hearts away from them toward Him. He shows us the emptiness in our cravings and the great joy of oneness with Him and with His children. He's the source and satisfaction of all our happiness. All we need is found in Him.

Remember that your strongest desires, the things that you are most passionate about, are what ultimately define your worship. If you passionately desire the respect of others, then your life will be colored by the fear of man. You'll worship other people's opinions. If you intensely crave acceptance, you'll be terrified of loneliness and rejection. You'll serve gods of man pleasing, peer pressure, or codependency.[22] If you covet comfort, pleasure, or fun, you'll worship money or prestige as gods who hold the power to bless or curse you.

---

20. I'm not saying that unbelievers are as wicked as they could be. Because of God's common grace, they are able to fulfill some of His design for them in their work and relationship, but their worship will always be sinfully self-focused. They will also have wrong motives behind their good works, but not all of them are as outwardly wicked as Hitler or Nero, for instance.

21. Col. 1:18 says that Jesus Christ "is also head of the body, the church; and He is the beginning . . . so that He Himself will come to have first place in everything."

22. See Ed Welch, *When People Are Big and God Is Small* (Phillipsburg, NJ: P&R, 1997).

Fig. 8.2. Adam's Pre-Fall Desires and Jesus' Perfect Desires

Adam's God-Given Sinless Desires Glorified God and Mirrored His Image by	Jesus' Perfect Desires Glorified God and Mirrored His Image by[23]
Ruling over creation, thereby bringing honor and respect to God and joy to himself.	Showing that He ruled over creation, thereby bringing honor and respect to His Father.
Physically becoming one with his spouse to enhance unity and joy. Producing children who would love and worship God.	Becoming a Man and reproducing Himself in disciples who would fill the earth with fruit through His bride, the church.
Subduing nature through joyful work accomplished for the pleasure of God.	Subduing all nature by His work and cultivating a field for His Father's pleasure.
Thankfully stewarding the resources of creation to sustain his and others' lives.	Depending upon His Father for His bodily needs. Meeting the true needs of others.
Enjoying the world by observing and classifying its beauty, design, and order.	Working so that the beauty and order in His Father would be seen in and by others.
Happily engaging in a time of rest and fellowship with his Creator and with others, primarily on the Sabbath but also throughout all of life.	Worshiping Him on the Sabbath through prayer, fellowship, and works of mercy.
Using communication to become one with his spouse so that they, together, would complete all of God's work, find joy in their differences, and please him.	Communicating with His bride, the church, and laying down His life for her. Bestowing upon her diverse gifts so that she might complete the building of His Kingdom.
Joining with others to complete the work God has assigned them for their mutual benefit and fellowship.	Enjoying fellowship and relationship with people and founding the church.
Glorifying and enjoying God in everything for his own good and God's pleasure.	Being One with Him in purpose and love by always doing the things that pleased Him.

23. Jesus' prayer in John 17 is a perfect reflection of each of these points.

As those who are being remade in God's likeness,[24] we must examine every longing in the blazing light of the Word of God. We must not be conformed to this world's philosophies—philosophies that would seductively lie to us about our true needs. Instead we must be "transformed by the renewing of [our minds]" (Rom. 12:2), so that we may know God's will and design for us.

Giving All Your Desires to Him

As we complete our discussion of our desires, let me remind you again about Hannah. She had strong desires; she longed to be happy and know the joy of motherhood. But by faith she sought God as the source of her happiness. She was willing to place all her desires on the altar of His will. Because she did so, she knew the pleasure of watching her son serve the Lord, who was her chief joy. But even Samuel, her son, wasn't the true son she was longing for. Samuel was a good priest, but Hannah (and all the rest of us) needed the true Prophet, Priest, and King whose miraculous birth would satisfy another mother's cry for salvation: "My soul magnifies the Lord, and my spirit rejoices in God my Savior, for he has looked on the humble estate of his servant. . . . For he who is mighty has done great things for me, and holy is his name" (Luke 1:46–49 esv).

God will answer your prayer for salvation and deliverance, just as He answered Hannah's. As you wrestle in prayer with your desires, may He grant you the grace to place them all on the altar of His love and service. It will then be your joy to watch His work in your life. He'll use your God-given desires to enliven, ignite, and compel your worship, your relationships, and your work for His glory.

24. "And put on the new self, which in the likeness of God has been created in righteousness and holiness of the truth" (Eph. 4:24).

FOR FURTHER THOUGHT

1. What would it be to desire God alone? See Psalm 42:1–2; 143:6; Isaiah 26:8–9; Luke 9:23–25.

2. Use a concordance to discover God's desires, joys, or delights, and write out the ones that are most precious to you. God's joy rests in fellowship with Himself and with His people. How does this change your view of God?

3. What does John 8:44 say about the source of ungodly desires? How does believing the truth as discussed in the last chapter play into our desires?

4. Prayerfully question yourself: What do you desire and long for? Is this a holy desire that's in the right place? Is it a holy desire that's too important to you? Does Jesus occupy the first place in this desire? In other words, are you willing to give it up for Him?

5. Is there anything on this list that you aren't willing to sacrifice to God? Can you see how this desire may function as a god for you?

9

Willing to Obey

*Who is the man who fears the LORD? He will instruct
him in the way he should choose. (Psalm 25:12)*

Mary of Bethany is one of the only people Jesus publicly commended for her making a godly choice. It isn't that no one else has chosen to follow the Lord—it's just that she's the only one who has been honored in this way. Jesus said that Mary had "chosen the good part" (Luke 10:42).

Mary's choice to sit at Jesus' feet was part of her character. On three different occasions, she chose to humble herself before Him. Once she sat on the floor at His feet, listening to Him, while her sister fumed in the kitchen. On another occasion, after Lazarus died, she fell at His feet, weeping in grief. Then, after Lazarus's resurrection, she humbled herself again and anointed Jesus' feet with costly spikenard (John 12:3).

One of the duties required by the first commandment in the Larger Catechism is "to worship and glorify Him by choosing Him." Why did Mary choose to sit at the Lord's feet while Martha complained? What was it about serving that so appealed to Martha that she chose to fuss with the Lord?

What Is the Will?

The will is the function of our heart or inner person that chooses. We use the term *will* numerous ways, such as "self-willed," "strong-willed," "free will," or "willpower." When we use *will* these ways, we're recognizing that people make choices and are known by the choices they make. Even hearts of children are known by their choices (Prov. 20:11). Why are some children strong-willed? Is it their environment? their personality? Why do other people seem weak-willed? Why do some will to worship God while others adamantly refuse to worship Him?

In this discussion about the will, we're going to see how our desires determine our choices and how God works upon the will.

Jonathan Edwards defined the will as "that by which the mind chooses anything. . . . An act of the will is the same as an act of choosing or choice."[1] Edwards writes further, "An act of the will is commonly expressed by its pleasing a man to do thus or thus; and a man doing as he wills, and doing as he pleases, are the same thing."[2]

The will is that faculty within us that decides whether we're having vanilla or chocolate, whether we're going to read our Bible or watch television. The will follows our thoughts and desires by choosing whatever we think will please us or afford us the best chance of happiness. It determines if we're going to seek to worship the Lord, as Mary did, or chase after other gods. If you're like me, you long for the day when you'll consistently choose the Lord.

Adam's Choice

From the beginning of recorded time, God placed a choice before mankind. The choice in the garden and the one we face today are the same: "Will you choose to worship and glorify Me or yourself?" All through history, in every time and place, God has commanded man to make the choice between Him or the world, the

---

1. Jonathan Edwards, *Freedom of the Will* (Morgan, PA: Soli Deo Publications, 1996), 1.
2. Ibid., 3.

flesh, and the Devil. In each of the following verses, believers are commanded to choose the Lord:

So choose life in order that you may live. (Deut. 30:19)

Choose for yourselves today whom you will serve: whether the gods which your fathers served. (Josh. 24:15)

How long will you hesitate between two opinions? If the LORD is God, follow Him; but if Baal, follow him. (1 Kings 18:21)

Choose what pleases Me. (Isa. 56:4)

It's evident that God has placed before us a choice: we can choose what pleases God (and ultimately gain true pleasure), or we can foolishly choose our way and gain immediate, though brief, pleasure.

New Year's Resolutions

How do you spend New Year's Day? Aside from trying to recover from a very late night, many spend at least part of the day making New Year's resolutions. Christians make New Year's resolutions along these lines: "This year I'm going to read my Bible all the way through." "This year I'm going to have a daily time of prayer." "This year I'm going to do better with my witnessing." Perhaps after reading this book you've said, "This year I'm going to seek to worship God alone." How do you do with your New Year's resolutions?

Once my friends and I decided to memorize a long Scripture passage. Although we did memorize part of it, our resolve petered out before Thanksgiving. Even though it didn't seem like it, I recognize that I made a deliberate choice not to memorize the Word. This choice followed the inclination of my heart, which is pretty apathetic when it comes to arduous discipline. I'm not saying that I never choose to discomfort myself, but it's a continual struggle, and I'm aware of the weakness of my will. Am I alone in this?

Considering the history of mankind, I doubt it. It doesn't take a great historian to see that aside from a few notable exceptions, man typically chooses to serve himself. Man always chooses according to his selfish desires. Edwards writes, "The heart never does choose the right, nor make a choice freed from self-love."[3] We can observe this truth because choosing to wholeheartedly love God and neighbor is not something mankind is famous for.

Joshua knew of mankind's inability to choose rightly. "You will not be able to serve the LORD, for He is a holy God," he said (Josh. 24:19). Does his sentiment surprise you? Joshua knew what the people were like—he knew that they wouldn't choose to worship God. He knew that they were self-centered and loved idolatry. Even though they proudly proclaimed that they would serve Him and obey His voice, history is clear what their true thoughts and desires were. It's plain that apart from God's gracious work in our hearts, we are just like them. We will always choose to serve ourselves and our gods. We too proclaim, "We will serve the Lord," then turn from Him.

Unruly Wills?

What is the problem? Why do we say one thing and do another? Are our wills dysfunctional? In one way, the answer to that question is yes. Our wills don't function in the way they should because God created the will to choose Him, but sin has damaged this

3. James M. Houston, ed., *Religious Affections: A Christian Character before God* (Minneapolis: Bethany House, 1996), xviii.

ability. Even though we've been given new hearts, including a will that is able to choose rightly, there still remains a strong influence of sin. Left to ourselves, in our own strength, even Christians still choose sinfully. We recognize that we were "brought forth in iniquity" (Ps. 51:5).

In spite of our fallenness, our wills are doing what they were created to do. It is not the will that is out of sync with the heart when we say we want to worship the Lord and then worship other gods. It is our words that are at variance with our strongest desires and inclinations.[4] Our will is working properly. It is choosing according to our dearest thoughts and desires. But, because of its sinful bent, our will is more strongly drawn to sin than to holiness. The difference between what we say ("We will serve the Lord") and what we do (serve ourselves) is not because of our wills per se. Our wills are functioning the way they were meant to. The contradiction is between our words ("We will serve the Lord") and our strongest desires. Our wills follow after the erroneous thoughts and sinful desires we delight in. Edwards puts it this way, "A man never, in any instance, wills anything contrary to his desires, or desires anything contrary to his will."[5]

Why do we profess great love for the Lord on Sunday morning and exaggerate our successes to our boss on Monday morning? Because we have divided desires. We have a God-given desire to work for God's glory (as seen in Adam) and a sinful desire to be respected and approved of. So when we're standing in front of our boss on Monday morning, the desire that is strongest (in this case, the desire to be respected) is what our will acts on when given a choice between telling the truth and exaggerating.

4. Jesus described the Pharisees with Isaiah's words, "This people honors Me with their lips, but their heart is far away from Me" (Matt. 15:8).

5. Jonathan Edwards, *Freedom of the Will*, ed. Harry S. Stout and Paul Ramsey, Revised Edition., vol. 1, The Works of Jonathan Edwards (New Haven; London: Yale University Press, 2009), 139.

Even though God has given us new hearts upon which He has written His law, our hearts are still contaminated by the lies and allurements of the world. That's why we say one thing and do another. If you wonder why you choose to worship other gods rather than wholeheartedly devote yourself to the Lord you love, examine the thoughts and desires that captivate your heart. That's where you'll find the answer to every sin and failure in your life. Don't be deceived into thinking that you need to develop more willpower. We don't need more "will power" or self-discipline. Rather, we need to develop godly thoughts and desires.

Wills Habituated to Sin

Our wills choose moment by moment to sin by following our deceived thoughts and self-aggrandizing desires. We also form habits of doing so. It's because of these habits that without much forethought our wills respond sinfully in certain circumstances. For instance, have you ever found yourself saying something that shocked you? I have. I wonder, "Where did that come from? Why did I say that?"

When something shocking comes out of my mouth, I wonder, "What's going on here? Did my will pull a fast one on me?" No, my will is functioning the way it should. I responded as I did because I habitually thought these thoughts, and my strongest desire was to give voice to them. It's just that now I'm surprised because they have come out of my mouth. We all have patterns of habitually choosing to sin in our thoughts and actions. The will becomes so accustomed to choosing in certain ways that it becomes second nature.

Not only do we consciously choose to sin; we habitually do so. If it's your practice to lie when you're under pressure, then you'll find yourself doing so even when it's not a conscious choice. If you always eat chocolate when you're feeling sorry for yourself, then if there's chocolate around and you're feeling badly, you'll go for it. If it's your habit to demand that others submit to you, then when your authority is challenged, you'll become angry and harsh. It's in this way that we serve other gods without being aware of it.

We've all had the experience of regretting something that at the time we were barely conscious of doing. Please don't misunderstand me. I'm not saying that we're not culpable for sinning in habitual ways, because we are. These sinful habits were originally formed by a conscious choice to ignore God and His law, so we are responsible, even though we're not always deliberately choosing to sin at that moment.

Free Will?[6]

Americans value freedom. We think that we, of all people, have a God-given right to choose to do whatever we want. The thought that I'm not the captain of my soul is so foreign and absurd as to be almost laughable. I'm not going to tell you that you don't have a free will. I'm not going to tell you that you don't possess the ability to freely choose according to your thoughts, inclinations, and desires, because it's obvious that every person always freely chooses what pleases him.

If we weren't able to freely choose what we wanted, then we would not be responsible for our choices. The problem is not that our will isn't free, it is that our desires are fallen. The problem lies in the focus of our heart. The Bible says that before we became

---

6. The main purpose of this book is not to convince you of either Calvinism or Arminianism. I'm sure that if your thought runs in either of those streams, you already know what I believe to be true. But it's also possible that unless you've consciously chosen to pursue an understanding of the issue and concept of free will, you might be wondering why I would talk about it. I need to talk about it now, at least briefly, because the concept of our free choice is so important to our discussion of idolatry that I can't ignore it, although it's not my purpose to sidetrack this discussion.

Christians, our hearts weren't neutral. We were contrary to God. "The old sinful nature within us is against God," Paul wrote. "It never did obey God's laws and it never will" (Rom. 8:7 TLB).[7]

Before Christ brought us to Himself and changed us, we freely chose to follow our strongest desires and inclinations. Our heart was against or contrary to God. Unbelievers can't understand truth and never desire to obey it. Make no mistake: they freely choose to live that way. It is their choice to follow the fallen nature—and they love it. The unbeliever has no power to choose to believe, to choose to live righteously, but he does freely choose to follow his own heart.

Once a person becomes a Christian, he has liberty. Unlike his old self, whose choice was always bound and toward sin, he is now able to choose to sin or not sin. Both of those choices are a possibility. When his heart is so inclined, when he's convinced of the goodness of it, and when he longs for the Lord and the joy of bringing Him pleasure, he chooses to obey Him. He's no longer a slave to sin in the same way that he was before he was saved. Before he was saved there was only one possible outcome in every choice: he was going to sin. But now that he has a new heart, there are two possibilities. He can sin or not sin, freely choosing according to his desires.

As you see, the problem is not that we need to develop more willpower. The problem is that we need new thoughts, new inclinations, and new desires. We don't need to learn how to pull ourselves up by our bootstraps or "gut it out." We need to seek to replace our sinful desires with holy ones, and that will happen only in the context of the gospel. When we hear about all He's

---

7. "You brood of vipers, how can you, being evil, speak what is good? For the mouth speaks out of that which fills the heart" (Matt. 12:34); "But a natural man does not accept the things of the Spirit of God, for they are foolishness to him; and he cannot understand them, because they are spiritually appraised" (1 Cor. 2:14).

done for us, how graciously He's called us into relationship with Him, we will develop a love for God that will change our desires and make us want to obey. This love for God that transforms our choices only occurs in response to His prior love for us, when we remember how freely we've been loved and welcomed by Him. When God grants these new holy passions to us, we'll find that our will, which seemed so weak before, will joyfully comply. We will find that we now love Him because He "first loved us" (1 John 4:19), and from that love will flow a desire to serve and please Him.

The Battle Within

Paul recognized he had a problem with his will: he had competing desires and inclinations fighting to take ascendancy in his heart. In the same way, even though I now have a strong desire to worship God, I find myself worshiping idols instead. Paul talked about this dilemma:

> For what I am doing, I do not understand; for I am not practicing what I would like to do, but I am doing the very thing I hate. . . . For I know that nothing good dwells in me, that is, in my flesh; for the willing is present in me, but the doing of the good is not. (Rom. 7:15, 18)

Unlike the unbeliever, as a Christian I am free to sin and not sin. But I'm forced to recognize that, like Paul, I have competing thoughts, inclinations, and desires that continually pull me in opposing directions. That's why striving for holiness is a never-ending war for the believer. You'll have to ceaselessly crush the unbelief and idols you find in your heart. And just when you think you've killed one, it will pop back up in another form. You will have to continue to remind yourself of how you've already been loved, already been forgiven, already been adopted, all because Jesus perfectly desired to love His Father and His neighbor above all things. And then you'll have to struggle to believe that this is what is most true about you. Your sin nature, which will continually question God's love, His goodness, His kind disposition toward you, will persistently fight against your faith in His love for you. And without faith in His benevolence toward you, you won't have the courage to get up and fight again . . . and again . . . and again. Your heart will continually ask, "How can God keep loving me? I know He must be angry . . ." And it's that very thought that will cause you to just give in and stop warring.

How many times have you wondered, "Why is being holy such a battle? It seems I start to get things right, and then all my good intentions go flying out the window. Why can't I get over this (whatever *this* is) and start living the way I know God wants me to"[8] The answer to that question is the same for you as for Paul. We have hearts that are torn between the love and worship of God and the love and worship of the world.[9] We believe the good news and yet are unbelievers. This war is marked out in the following verses. See if you can pick out the competing loves:

> If anyone comes to Me, and does not hate his own father and mother and wife and children and brothers and sisters, yes, and even his own life, he cannot be My disciple. Whoever does not carry his own cross and come after Me cannot be My disciple. (Luke 14:26–27)

8. Because many Christians don't understand how the will functions or even that they have competing desires, they become frustrated with their growth and look for other unbiblical answers to their dilemma.

9. Only God has complete and unfettered liberty to do as He pleases. "But our God is in the heavens; He does whatever He pleases" (Ps. 115:3); "Whatever the LORD pleases, He does, in heaven and in earth, in the seas and in all deeps" (Ps. 135:6). See also 1 Sam. 3:18; Job 23:13; Pss. 33:9–11; 46:10–11; Dan. 4:35; Matt. 11:25–26; Acts 4:28; Eph. 1:11; Phil. 2:10–11. Take note of the fact that God does whatever He pleases—whatever brings pleasure to Him.

If I were still trying to please men, I would not be a bond-servant of Christ. (Gal. 1:10)

You adulteresses, do you not know that friendship with the world is hostility toward God? Therefore whoever wishes to be a friend of the world makes himself an enemy of God. (James 4:4)

Do not love the world nor the things in the world. If anyone loves the world, the love of the Father is not in him. (1 John 2:15)

Even as believers, with new hearts and renewed desires, it is impossible that any of us will perfectly love God with our whole heart, soul, mind, and strength because of remaining sin and our unbelief. Our hearts will always be drawn away to things we can see, taste, and touch, drawn away to something more than faith in the unseen. We will always be tempted to choose to worship something other than God, to love something more than we love Him, to swear our allegiance to other deities—whether to ourselves as our own savior or to someone or something else we think has the power to make us truly happy.

If it seems to you that you've sought to make those choices before, to no avail, remember you're fighting a war, not just a little skirmish. You can rejoice because the Lord Jesus has already triumphed over your sin on the cross, and one day you will be completely free. But at the same time, you can seek to guard against the deceptive thoughts, desires, or inclinations of your heart. You can fight against unbelief and continually throw yourself on the mercy of God. Even so, you'll constantly be enticed by the love of self, money, family, possessions, man's good opinion, the world, and the things in it . . . even when you've made up your mind to worship God alone.

God has placed within every true Christian a desire to choose Him. We all long to hear Him say, "Well done, good and faithful servant. . . . Enter into the joy of your master" (Matt. 25:23 ESV), don't we? Of course, we know that Jesus was the only truly good, truly faithful servant and that the joy we will ultimately enter into is the joy that he has earned for us. But even though we long to be fully obedient, none of us consistently chooses the path of that good and faithful slave. Why did Joshua tell the Israelites that in spite of all their good intentions they weren't going to be able to serve Him? The truth about the choices we make is plain. We don't consistently choose the Lord because we don't really desire Him . . . and we don't really desire Him because we're not convinced that He really loves us and that in that love we will find our ultimate happiness.

Let's face it: we're glutted on the joys and pleasures of the world,[10] and our minds remain unconvinced that the joy that the Master has generously bestowed on us is all that much better. "The attractions of this world and the delights of wealth, and the search for success and lure of nice things" (Mark 4:19 TLB) crowd out love for God. Remember the mud pies C. S. Lewis spoke of? We choose to play in the slum because we're satisfied with mud and it seems better than our other options.

At this point, like Paul, we may cry out, "Wretched man that I am! Who will set me free from the body of this death?" His answer? "Thanks be to God through Jesus Christ our Lord!" (Rom. 7:24–25). It is God who can set us free and change us through the work that has already been accomplished by His Son on our behalf. On our own, our position would be utterly hopeless, but because He's committed Himself to work in us (and His work is never thwarted), we can be encouraged.

---

10. Even if that joy is derived from self-pity or peace at any price, it still comes from a love of the world and is a joy in doing things your way.

God's Work in Your Will

When Paul encouraged the Philippians to "work out" their salvation with fear and trembling (Phil. 2:12), he pointed them to the only hope that they had of accomplishing it: God's faithful and prior work. "For it is God who is at work in you, both to will and to work for His good pleasure" (2:13). That God is willing to continue to work in us all that He desires is our only hope. Our growth in holiness is in His hands, and we can rest while at the same time we labor, knowing that He is committed to accomplishing the transformation of our hearts that we long for . . . all in His own time . . . as we cooperate in faith.

God accomplishes this work in you by changing your thoughts, desires, and inclinations that give rise to your choices. He does so by continually convincing you that you are already loved and already forgiven. His love *will* produce love in you, and this love *will* transform your desires. Because you are loved, you no longer need to justify yourself or prove that you're really okay after all. His work is to cause you to believe; your work is to respond in faith to all He's done for you and to continue to war against your unbelief.

Mary's Excellent Choice

What should we say about Mary's excellent choices? Did she make those choices because she had a strong will and was very self-disciplined? Was she naturally holy or good-natured? Yes, she made a conscious decision to worship her Lord, but her decision wasn't based on her self-discipline or "gutting it out for the Lord." Her decisions flowed out of a love for Jesus, a love that had been born and cultivated in her by His continual welcome and love for her. She had a desire to be with Jesus, to abase herself before Him, to give Him the most precious gift she had, because she was convinced that she was fully loved by Him. Her will was prompted to worship Him because her heart was captivated by Him . . . she could do nothing less. Of course, her belief in His love for her was sorely tried when her brother, Lazarus, died—yet she continued to believe and ultimately anointed the Savior she loved for His burial (John 12).

It was God's sovereign choice to work in Mary as He did, convincing her of Jesus' love, making her hungry for Him. His plan for Mary was that she would be known as a woman who worshiped Him and chose rightly. If we believe in anything other than God's sovereign rule over our hearts, then we are left without hope for change. If Mary chose the way she did because she was a better person than Martha, then what hope is there for the rest of us, who know that we're not that good? What's to become of those of us who know that our worship is polluted and that we don't really hate our sin as we should? What about those of us who have never consistently worshiped God? What about those of us who were reared as unbelievers or who have habitual ungodly desires that dominate us? If we rely on anything other than the sovereign grace of God to transform us, then we're doomed to a life of continual comparison and defeat. God has promised to work in us. It is our wisdom to believe that His plan for us is good, even if that plan means that we are to struggle for a season while He purifies our desires. As His beloved children, we can rest in the glorious truth that God can so work upon our hearts that we will yearn for Him more than anything else. He can direct our hearts to worship Him, just as surely as He directed Mary's heart.

Proverbs 21:1 says, "The king's heart is like channels of water in the hand of the LORD; He turns it wherever He wishes."[11] Humanly speaking, no one has more power to freely choose to do

11. See also Ezra 7:27–28; Neh. 1:11; 2:4; Pss. 105:25; 106:46; Prov. 16:1, 9; 20:24; Dan. 4:35; Acts 7:10; Rom. 8:29; Eph. 1:3–4.

whatever he wants than a king. But even a king's authority means nothing when it comes to God's sovereign choice. In the same way that God turns the hearts of great men, He can turn your heart to worship Him. So rest in Him . . . rejoicing in His great love and effectual power. He can accomplish all His work in you. Instead of worshiping Mary and others we admire in the Bible, we can wholeheartedly worship God and say of Him, "Isn't He good? I want to love Him as He has loved me."

FOR FURTHER THOUGHT

1. What are the three functions of the heart? How are they interrelated?

2. How strong is your willpower and self-discipline?

3. What is the relationship between your choices and your desires?

4. Can you pinpoint areas in your life in which you habitually choose to serve God? yourself? What desires motivate these choices?

5. Rewrite the following verses in your words and then pray them to the Lord. Plead with Him that He would grant you holy desires.
   a. Psalm 63:1–5
   b. Psalm 42:1–2
   c. Psalm 73:25–28
   d. Psalm 119:20, 81
   e. Psalm 143:6
   f. Isaiah 26:8–9

10

Resisting Your Idols

Put off your old self, which is being corrupted
by its deceitful desires. (Ephesians 4:22 NIV)

Change is difficult, isn't it? As I write this, workmen are digging up my backyard. Although I ordered this work, watching them tear up my lovely green grass and get mud everywhere is distressing. That's because I enjoyed my yard the way it was. Even though I want this work, I have to admit I hate the process of change. I have to keep reminding myself I'm the one who caused all this mess and hope the results will bring me more happiness than the process is.

In some ways, that's how it is with the change God works in us. All Christians want to be changed. They long to be holy. You wouldn't have gotten this far in this book if you weren't sincere about getting rid of your idols and developing pure worship. We experience fear, though, when we realize this change will cause discomfort. I'm sure in many ways our transformation into holiness will be more uncomfortable than watching my little yard get demolished.

Sanctification: God's Method of Change

One of the great weaknesses in modern Christianity is a misconception of how change is achieved in a believer's heart. This change is referred to in the New Testament as sanctification. Sanctification is both positional and progressive. Positional sanctification is that instantaneous change wrought in us by the Spirit when He declares us "holy and blameless." In this sense, every Christian is wholly sanctified. On the other hand, progressive sanctification is the slow process of change whereby God transforms our hearts into His image and likeness. Progressive sanctification is God's method to make us inwardly what we already are positionally. God's Spirit works graciously, progressively, and relentlessly in us because it is His will to make us both completely loving and completely free.

We shouldn't think that progressive sanctification is like a ride up an escalator, though. It is not a straight, diagonally vertical line. No, frequently it looks more like a scribble from a crayon than a precise trajectory upward. Sometimes it will seem as though we're progressing along just fine only to find ourselves back where we started. We need to remember that progressive sanctification, like positional sanctification, is in God's hands and that He will use both our successes and our failures, our growth and our falls, for His purposes and glory.

We also need to know that progress in holiness is not measured by outward works (what we start and stop doing), although it is not usually less than that. True holiness is not measured by outward behavior but by inward love, love for God and love for our neighbor. Yes, this love will produce a change in words and deeds, but it is not just measured by adherence to the commands, "Do not taste," "Do not touch" (Col. 2:21). It is best defined as "faith working through love" (Gal. 5:6).

Although the exact means God uses to transform us is unique to each of us, the general process is the same for all Christians. This process is outlined most clearly (although it's seen all through Scripture) in Ephesians 4:22–24 (NIV):

> You were taught, with regard to your former way of life, to put
> off your old self, which is being corrupted by its deceitful de-

sires; to be made new in the attitude of your minds; and to put on the new self, created to be like God in true righteousness and holiness.

Can you identify the three steps that make up the process of progressive sanctification? The first step is "put off your old self." The second step is "be made new in the attitude of your minds." And the third step is "put on the new self." Rather than looking at these steps as sequential—one being done before the next is begun—look at them as simultaneous. At the same time that we seek to put off our old self, the Spirit will renew our attitude and enable us put on new habits that mirror God's righteousness and holiness.

God's method of change involves negative (put off) and positive (put on) aspects as the Spirit transforms our faith, our thinking, and desires. True sanctification is a combination of both facets. For instance, it isn't enough to merely stop or put off the worship of our false gods. We have to put on worship and love of the living God while our attitudes are being renewed by the Spirit.

In this chapter we'll look at the first step, "put off," remembering that these are not crisp mathematical equations but rather brush strokes in an artist's rendering of a beautiful landscape (like my backyard used to be).

Fighting Sin before It Begins

Putting off sin begins with fighting temptation when it first arises. Becoming more aware of the origin and process of temptation will help us put off old idolatrous habit patterns—before we fall into them.

What Is Temptation?
Temptation is a common experience to all. Both God and Satan are involved in our trials and temptations, though with greatly differing

goals. God tries or tests[1] His children out of great love for them. He does this so they will grow in their knowledge of His character and in their need for reliance upon Him. God's activity in testing and trying us leads to good—our good and His glory. He tests us so that we will come to know that He is truly as merciful as He says He is.

By contrast, Satan has evil as his goal. God never leads us into evil because He never entices us to spurn His glory and pleasure. Satan's temptation is his work to cause us to sin. Satan attacks us by insinuating that God doesn't really love us, that He isn't really wise, and that He's not really powerful. Then, after we succumb to his lies, he accuses us and tells us that God never really loved us and that now we've fallen so badly that nothing will ever make Him love us again.

The Devil's temptation occurs in our hearts in concert with the influences of the world and our fleshly natures. The lies of the world and our deceitful thoughts and desires are useful tools in his attack. Satan uses two powerful weapons in this attack: the first is fear and the second is pleasure. He tempts us through fear by suggesting that obedience to God will result in the loss of something we believe we must have in order to be happy. At the same time he tempts us through pleasure by portraying the joys that disobedience will bring us. He frightens us with thoughts that God isn't really good and loving; he entices us with thoughts of how we might as well look for any avenue to please ourselves. But make no mistake, his temptation does not put anything into us that is not there already. We succumb to Satan's temptations because of the lusts that already live in our hearts.

Let's look at three examples of temptation from Scripture: Judas, Peter, and Christ. All three of these men were tempted, but

---

1. See Gen. 22:1–2; 2 Chron. 32:31; 2 Cor. 12:9; 1 Peter 1:5–7; Deut. 13:3.

with significantly different results. Do you know why Judas's and Peter's temptation ended in sin? Do you know why Christ was able to resist? Do you understand why you fall to some temptations while others hold no attraction for you?

Judas's Temptation

When Satan tempted Judas, he was successful because it was in Judas's character to love money.[2] Judas was already an idolater. He loved money more than he loved the Lord, so it wasn't much of a stretch to betray Jesus for thirty pieces of silver. Judas was easy prey for Satan's attack because his love for the Lord was overshadowed by his love for the prestige and respect that money brings. Like Rachel before him, his idolatry turned out to be the snare that brought on his ultimate destruction. Satan planted the fear in his heart that Christ would never oust the Romans while at the same time enticing him with thoughts of the pleasure that thirty pieces of silver would bring. Judas thought he would be a man worthy of love and respect if he could force Christ's hand into grasping the kingdom for Himself. He believed in justification by power and riches.

Peter's Temptation

Satan was successful in tempting Peter because the desire to protect himself and be liked was already ruling in his life. He could have resisted Satan's temptation to deny the Lord if he really was ready to "lay down" his life for Him as he claimed. Satan's temptation of Peter was effective because, though Peter might have been willing to die for Him, he didn't yet desire to suffer for Him. Satan caused Peter to fear the censure that loyalty to Christ brings while

2. Satan was also successful because God had chosen Judas to be the one to betray Him. Satan can never be successful in any of his devious schemes without the permission of the sovereign King of heaven (see Job 1:6–12; 2:1–6).

enticing him to imagine the pleasure of his own safety. Peter believed in justification by safety.

Why didn't Peter end up like Judas, dangling at the end of a rope? Was his character stronger or better? Peter didn't despair utterly because Jesus prayed for Him. Although Peter's faith was weak, it was impossible for it to fail utterly because it was securely kept in the Lord's hand.

> Simon, Simon, behold, Satan has demanded permission to sift you like wheat; but I have prayed for you, that your faith may not fail; and you, when once you have turned again, strengthen your brothers. (Luke 22:31–32)

There was no question Peter would face Satan's attack. God had already granted Satan permission to assault him. There was no question Peter was going to fall. The Lord knew Peter's heart. He knew his thoughts and desires (John 2:24–25). Unless His Father intervened, Peter would freely choose to follow his strongest inclination right into sin. Jesus wasn't shocked by Peter's denial. In fact He allowed it so that Peter would grow in holiness. Can you see how even in Peter's sin God is glorified and we are encouraged in our battle?

Have you been gripped by the truth that Jesus has promised to keep you through your failures? Do you believe that even though you fall, your faith will not completely fail? Though you might "weep bitterly" over sin, you can rejoice that God is stronger than your heart (1 John 3:19–20). His Spirit can conquer your most formidable fears and dearest pleasures and keep you safe.

The Temptation of Our Lord

Satan's temptation of Christ was a different story. Jesus would never succumb to Satan's temptations because it was His sole desire to please His Father. That's why He said of Satan, "He has nothing in Me. . . . I do exactly as the Father commanded Me" (John 14:30–31). Satan found no handhold in Jesus' heart. His only thought and desire was to please and rejoice in His Father. He was able to conquer Satan because He had a sinless heart—his thoughts, desires, affections, and motivations were all focused "like a flint" on pleasing Him (Luke 9:51). He had already lived thirty years in complete submission to and love for His Father. He harbored no fear except that of offending the Father whom He loved.

> My Father, if it is possible, let this cup pass from Me; yet not as I will, but as You will. (Matt. 26:39)

> Jesus said to them, "My food is to do the will of Him who sent Me and to accomplish His work." (John 4:34)

> I do not seek My own will, but the will of Him who sent Me. (John 5:30; see also John 6:38; 8:29; 15:10; Matt. 3:17; 17:5)

Jesus didn't give in to Satan's attacks because His heart was focused exclusively on loving His Father. He wasn't afraid of missing worldly pleasures because He didn't desire anything but His Father's smiling countenance.

The Temptation in the Wilderness

Rejoice that you are not alone in your struggle against sin. You have a High Priest who was tempted as you are and yet overcame. Jesus resisted Satan's temptation in the wilderness to satisfy His hunger because He loved relying on His Father's provision. He wasn't afraid He would starve to death or be too weak to obey. He rejoiced in the strength that came from obedience to His Word. He resisted Satan's temptation to test His Father's love by casting Himself off a high peak, because He didn't need to prove anything to Satan. He didn't desire Satan's good opinion or fear losing his approval. He was able to resist the Devil's temptation to worship him even though He had been promised all the "kingdoms of the world and their glory" (Matt. 4:8). He was triumphant because He didn't desire anything the world had to offer: not riches, fame, or power. He knew happiness was found in His Father's smile alone. He didn't need to justify Himself.

The second great temptation of Christ came in the garden of Gethsemane. There He wrestled with His holy desires to please His Father and to be one with Him. He knew that in order to fully satisfy His Father's will, He would have to be the Sin Bearer. The sweet union He had with His Father from all time would be severed for a season as He drank down the sin He had shunned His whole life. How His soul must have agonized over the thought of being separated from His Father. If He was ever tempted to fear, this must have been the time. Although He was aware of the physical pain and torture to come, His torment in the garden sprang from His realization that for the first time in all eternity He would experience the ultimate effect of sin: alienation from His Father. What a fearful prospect that must have been!

Do you see the sympathy and aid available to you? You struggle with strong desires to worship other gods, but they are faint in comparison with the holy desire Christ anguished over as He faced the separation that the cross would bring. He loved the oneness He had with His Father.[3] He longed to please Him and bring Him joy above all else. Yet He sacrificed His desire so that He might ultimately please Him and redeem you.

Rejoice because your victorious Savior is standing by you, ready to aid you in your struggle against sin.

---

3. Matt. 11:27; 28:19; John 1:1–2; 5:17, 23; 8:58; 14:9, 23; 16:15; 17:10, 21. His statement, "I and the Father are one" (John 10:30), was more than a statement of truth. It was a statement of His nature, His joy, His purpose in being.

For since He Himself was tempted in that which He has suffered, He is able to come to the aid of those who are tempted. (Heb. 2:18)

For we do not have a high priest who cannot sympathize with our weaknesses, but One who has been tempted in all things as we are, yet without sin. (Heb. 4:15)

Will you be able to grow in overcoming sinful desires? Yes, in part, but not by your willpower or self-discipline. You will overcome only in the power of your risen Savior and through the realization of your justification. You will overcome by the good news of the gospel: His blood and your testimony about His grace for you (Rev. 12:11). Your justification means not only that He no longer counts you guilty for your sin but also that He has transferred His record of victory over temptation to you. He prioritized His desires and conquered fear on your behalf, and—praise Him!—that's your record today if you believe. In the same way that Christ strengthened Peter and kept his faith from failing in spite of his sin, He will strengthen you because you are precious to Him, because you are His dearly loved bride. Just knowing that He doesn't hold your failures against you and that the Father doesn't accuse you of succumbing to Satan's whims is a strong help in your ongoing struggle. Yes, we are terribly flawed, but even so, we are wonderfully loved.

What Are You Tempted to Worship?

Satan is successful in tempting us to sin because we have idolatrous thoughts and desires. That's why it's so important to become aware of them. Remember that fear of loss and imaginations of pleasure spring from our idolatrous desires, and it is those desires that make us easy prey for our enemy.

We can become more aware of the thoughts and desires that ensnare us by asking, What do I want and fear? Or, to put a finer point on it, What do I want and fear more than I want to reflect God and grow in holiness? What pleasure do you want so badly that you're willing to sin in order to obtain it? What do you fear losing so much that you think nothing of sinning in order to hang on to it?

Sometimes it's difficult to answer these questions immediately, so I'll furnish you with a helpful exercise.

Think back to the last time that you know you sinned. This is important because of the relationship between your functional gods (idols) and sinful behavior. Choose a sin that you habitually fall into, like anger, self-indulgence, or fear, for instance. Write this circumstance down.

With this circumstance in mind, ask God to help you answer the following questions. Try not to give one-word answers that don't plumb the depth of your thoughts, desires, and fears. Each of these questions will help you to understand your idolatry, so don't hurry through your answers. Instead, prayerfully ask God, the Heart Knower, to reveal your "functional gods" to you.[4]

1. What did you want, desire, or wish for?
2. What did you fear? What were you worrying about?
3. What did you think you needed?
4. What were your strategies and intentions designed to accomplish?
5. What or whom were you trusting?
6. Whom were you trying to please? Whose opinion of you counted?

---

4. These questions are adapted from Dave Powlison's "X-Ray Questions: Drawing Out the Why's and Wherefore's of Human Behavior," *The Journal of Biblical Counseling* 18, no. 1 (Winter 2001): 2.

7. What were you loving? Hating?

8. What would have brought you the greatest pleasure, happiness, or delight? What would have brought you the greatest pain and misery?

9. Were you remembering your Father's great love for you in Christ?

10. Were you convinced that you were already forgiven, already righteous, needing nothing?

Let me give you an example from my life that might help you to see how idolatry functions.[5] Recently I was asked by a friend to lead a Bible study in addition to my regular teaching schedule. At her request, I met with the class and presented what I considered the core of the lesson. Later, the friend who requested my help criticized me. I responded by becoming sinfully angry, gossiping about my friend's ingratitude and ignorance, and becoming defensive with her. I oscillated between self-righteousness (How dare she say these things about me?) and self-pity (I'm such a terrible person. I'll never change. I think I'll just quit teaching anyone.).

Sinful anger was a habitual problem in my life, and out of it flowed rivers of self-pity, gossip, self-indulgence, and hopelessness. Let's look now at how I might have answered the preceding questions.

1. *What did you want, desire, or wish for?* I wanted my friend's gratitude and good opinion. I wanted her to think well of me. I was justifying myself by serving her.

2. *What did you fear? What were you worrying about?* I feared that she didn't like me and didn't appreciate me. I feared that I couldn't be happy without her praise.

5. This example is easy for me to use because although it's contrived, I've played it out on many occasions.

3. *What did you think you needed?* Her respect and honor. I was trying to gain her approval.

4. *What were your strategies and intentions designed to accomplish?* In part, I was trying to serve the Lord, but I was also trying to improve her opinion of me.

5. *What or whom were you trusting?* I trusted that her approval could make me happy. I was also trusting in the Lord for the teaching, but this wasn't my primary focus, as is obvious by my reaction.

6. *Whom were you trying to please? Whose opinion of you counted?* Her opinion was most important to me. I was trying to please her but felt conflicted because I also wanted to teach the class the truth (which I knew wouldn't please her).

7. *What did you love? What did you hate?* I loved being respected. I hated the fact that my friend didn't appreciate me. I hated the thought that I might not be worthy of love or respect.

8. *What would have brought you the greatest pleasure, happiness, or delight? What would have brought you the greatest pain and misery?* Her approval would have brought me delight, and I experienced misery because I didn't have it. I was giving my friend the power to control my life by making her the source of my happiness.

9. *Were you remembering your Father's great love for you in Christ?* No. I was only thinking about how I needed her love. I was trying to justify myself through my relationship with her.

10. *Were you convinced that you were already forgiven, already righteous, needing nothing?* No, especially not when I fell into despair, assuming that I would never change and that God was certainly angry with me.

The reason I fell to the temptation to become sinfully angry was because my motives and desires were impure. I feared the loss of my friend's good opinion. I desired respect and praise. I sought to justify myself. Do you understand why it wouldn't be enough to ask God to forgive me just for being put out with my friend (although that would be appropriate)? It wouldn't suffice because my sin was deeper than the mere outer display of anger. My sin had its roots in my false worship. Because I was idolizing my friend's opinion of me, she functioned as a god in my life. I'm an idolater. She had the power to control my peace and joy. I longed for her blessing . . . I feared her curse. I feared that I couldn't approve of myself, that I really wasn't "okay" after all.

Understanding Temptation's Work

Let's examine how I fell into sin in light of James 1:13–16. James wrote,

> Let no one say when he is tempted, "I am being tempted by God"; for God cannot be tempted by evil, and He Himself does not tempt anyone. But each one is tempted when he is carried away and enticed by his own lust. Then when lust has conceived, it gives birth to sin; and when sin is accomplished, it brings forth death. Do not be deceived, my beloved brethren.

Although God tries us for our holiness, we can't blame God for our sin. I freely choose to sin in response to the thoughts, desires, and fears that rule me. Although God rules sovereignly in my life, I am fully responsible for my sin and can never blame Him.

I fell into temptation because I was "carried away and enticed" by my lusts. "As in . . . fishing the game is 'lured' from its haunt, so man's lust 'allures' him from the safety of his self-restraint."[6] Like a dumb fish, I gave into temptation when confronted with a big, juicy worm made up of the happiness I thought I would experience. What gave temptation power in my life? My loves, desires, and lusts!

Fig. 10.1. When the Heart Desires Pleasing Self

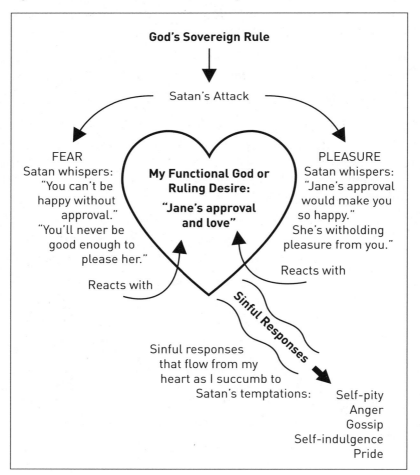

6. *Vine's Expository Dictionary of Biblical Words,* electronic database (Nashville: Thomas Nelson Publishers, 1985).

I can see how I'm tempted to desire my friend's good opinion in order to justify myself. Satan is successful in tempting me to sin when I'm involved with this friend because I value her opinion too highly. Her words control me because I think I need her approval to be happy. Instead of loving and serving her, I fear her and love her good opinion of me. When an opportunity comes along for me to be with her, I'm tempted by my lusts to sin. I wrongly believe that her approval is analogous to God's approval and my ultimate righteousness. Then when lust gains its goal, it gives birth to sin, and when sin is brought to full fruition, it brings forth death.

I've been deceived, and that deception has its roots in the desires or lusts resident in my heart. The deception is that I must play to her and please her in order to be happy. The truth is that I need only concern myself with the Audience of One. Those "who live before the Audience of One can say to the world: 'I have only one audience. Before you I have nothing to prove, nothing to gain, nothing to lose.'"[7] If I were playing only to the Audience of One, I could have responded in a more godly way to her criticism. In figure 10.2, observe how the desires of the heart can combat Satan's two-pronged temptation when it comes.

Judas was successfully tempted to betray Christ because he desired money, power, and prestige. He thought he would only have worth if he was on a winning team. Rachel was tempted to worship idols and be sinfully angry with Jacob because she wanted the respect and love that a child could bring her. She believed in justification by motherhood. Eli was successfully tempted to spoil his children because he wanted peace. Lot's wife was tempted to disobey the angels because she wanted the comforts of her home. Peter was tempted to deny Christ because he

7. Os Guinness, *The Call: Ending and Fulfilling the Central Purpose of Your Life* (Chicago: Moody Press, 1992), 77.

Fig. 10.2. When the Heart Desires Pleasing the Audience of One

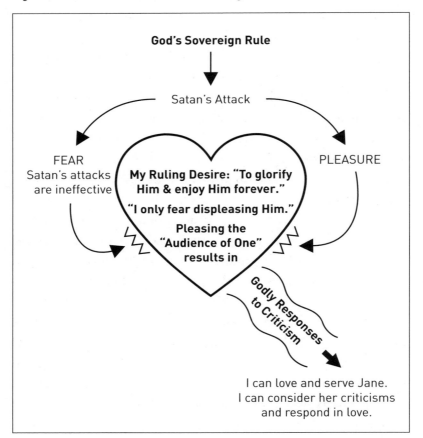

desired security and others' good opinions. He believed in justification by self-aggrandizement and safety. Martha was successfully tempted to bark at the Lord and fume at her sister because
she longed to be thought of as a gracious hostess. She believed
in justification by hospitality. The Pharisees were successfully
tempted to pursue Christ to the death because they loved the
"respectful greetings in the market places" (Matt. 23:7) and the
"place of honor at banquets" (Matt. 23:6) and were envious of
His position with the people. And I was successfully tempted to

sin by being angry with my friend because I loved my own glory more than I loved pleasing God.

"Lead Us Not"

What must we do to resist temptation and begin to put off our habitual idolatry?

We must put on purposeful prayer about our desires and the temptations that flow from them. Our Lord Jesus, who knew how to wrestle with temptation, has given us this counsel, "Pray, then, in this way. . . . 'Do not lead us into temptation, but deliver us from evil'" (Matt. 6:9, 13; see also Matt. 26:41; Luke 11:4; 22:46). When we pray in this way we aren't asking God not to tempt us, because we know that He never does. What we're asking is that He keep us from falling into sin's clutches. God does allow our faith to be tried, but with each trial He provides a way out so that we are never put in a position where sinning is our only option (1 Cor. 10:13). Because of this, we can have great hope in our battle against temptation. We must put on prayer specifically to be kept from giving in to our lusts and fears; that when they come along we'll be aware and armed against them; that He will supply the aid we need when we are faced with them. And we must pray that God would grant us holy desires and a proper fear of Him and that He would enable us to believe that His love for us is never ending.

Jesus warned His followers, "Keep watching and praying that you may not enter into temptation; the spirit is willing, but the flesh is weak" (Matt. 26:41).[8] As our Father's children, we desire to obey God. But we don't obey Him, because we are easily enticed by our fleshly nature (Rom. 7:25). We're weak. We're vulnerable

---

8. See also Luke 21:36; 1 Peter 4:7.

to attack. The only way to be successful against the schemes of the Devil is to be alert and to give ourselves to prayer. We must be on guard to consider the snares that could be used by our enemy to ensnare us. Peter warns his readers to "be of sober spirit, be on the alert. Your adversary, the devil, prowls around like a roaring lion, seeking someone to devour" (1 Peter 5:8).

It's in light of God's call to watch that I've tried to help you understand your areas of weakness. Satan will strike at the heart of your idolatry. He'll observe your words and actions, and he'll know what you long for more than holiness. He'll know what you fear. And it's there he'll attack you. He'll frighten you with the thought that you'll never be happy without your longed-for desire. He'll entice you with imaginations of the pleasures that could be yours if you give in to sin just this once. He'll remind you of all the ways you've already blown it and insinuate that God couldn't possibly love you anymore . . . that you've gone way too far and that you might as well just give in. Then you'll fall into sin—unless you're forearmed through prayer and diligent watchfulness.

God Knows How to Deliver You

The book of 2 Peter is written to those who were facing the temptation to give up in the face of great persecution and heresy. "The Lord knows how to rescue the godly from temptation" (2 Peter 2:9) are the Holy Spirit's words through Peter to us. As we wrestle with the idols in our hearts, we can rest assured that God hasn't forgotten how to preserve us, either. We must be watchful, we must pray, but it is, after all, up to our loving Father to protect and keep us. He can deliver us from temptation. He can rescue us from Satan's schemes, and He can even cause us to turn back to Him if we fall . . . all for His ultimate glory and pleasure.

Let's join the Puritans in praying,

O God, the Author of all good,
I come to thee for the grace that another day will require for its
duties and events.
    I step out into a wicked world,
    I carry about with me an evil heart,
    I know that without thee I can do nothing,
that everything with which I shall be concerned,
however harmless in itself,
may prove an occasion of sin or folly,
unless I am kept by thy power.
Hold thou me up and I shall be safe.
Preserve my understanding from subtlety of error,
    my affections from love of idols,
    my character from stain of vice,
    my profession from every form of evil.[9]

Ask the Lord to grant you the wisdom you need to fight temptation and put off idolatry. Ask Him to show you the thoughts and
desires that Satan uses to frighten and entice you and the ways in
which your enemy accuses both you and your Father. And, finally,
ask Him to help you put off any self-sufficiency, pride, and unbelief
that would stop you from watching and praying with a vigilant heart.

FOR FURTHER THOUGHT

1. Write out the differences between the temptations of Judas
   and Peter.

9. Arthur Bennett, *The Valley of Vision: A Collection of Puritan Prayers and Devotions*
(Carlisle, PA: Banner of Truth Trust, 1995), 118.

2. Why was Satan ineffective in his temptation of Christ?

3. Does God ever tempt us to evil? Why does He test or try us?

4. What is Satan's goal in tempting us?

5. What are the three steps in progressive sanctification?

6. How does overcoming temptation fit into the first step?

7. What are the two tools that Satan uses to tempt all believers to sin? What are the specific ones that he uses in your life?

8. In light of Christ's warning to watch against temptation, what should you be specifically concerned about? How will you put on dependent, watchful prayer?

11

Crushing Your False Gods

*If by the Spirit you are putting to death the deeds
of the body, you will live. (Romans 8:13)*

Three months after Israel's delivery from the hand of their Egyptian enemy, Moses ascended Mount Sinai to meet with God. While he tarried there for forty days, the children of Israel became fearful and impatient. They began to fear that he had died and they might be left without a leader. They forgot about the God who had delivered and sustained them in the wilderness. In their unbelief they thought their ultimate happiness hinged on Moses being around to deliver them. They didn't believe that God was able to bring them into the Promised Land with or without a Moses. They felt desperate—they needed a god they could trust, one they could see and feel, a god like the ones they had worshiped in Egypt (Deut. 32). Stephen hit the nail on the head: "In their hearts [they] turned back to Egypt" (Acts 7:39).

"We don't know what's happened to Moses. Make us a god who will lead us!" they cried to Aaron. Foolishly caving in to them, he responded, "Give me your gold earrings." Perhaps he feared that in their impatience they would be angry or rebel against him. He may have rationalized that a little idolatry was better than outright rebellion and desertion. Or perhaps he was concerned about Moses' whereabouts and thought a little help from a more tangible god wouldn't be so bad. In any case, he melted their gold jewelry and "molded and tooled it into the form of a calf" (Ex. 32:4 TLB). The people were thrilled to have a god that they could see, a god they could really trust. They exclaimed, "This is your god, O Israel, who brought you up from the land of Egypt" (Ex. 32:4). Think about the irony: Moses was on the mountain receiving the law while Aaron and the Israelites were fashioning gods and proclaiming, "This is the god that delivered us from Egypt!"

Moses returned quickly from the mountain when God told him about the people and their carousing. In terrible anger he smashed the tablets of the law before them in a visible display of what they had already done. Then Moses took the idol, the "sinful thing, the calf . . . and burned it with fire and crushed it, grinding it very small until it was as fine as dust; and . . . threw its dust into the brook that came down from the mountain" (Deut. 9:21).

Think about the differences between Moses and Aaron. Aaron was focused on pleasing the people, so he gave in to their desire for a god that would protect and lead them. He undoubtedly justified himself by thinking about the difficulty of leadership. Like Moses, he probably thought about his inability to lead such a stubborn group. He may have thought that although his actions were wrong, they were excusable. His desire to be popular among the people resulted in great sin and loss for many that day.

How was it possible for Satan to tempt Aaron in this way? Hadn't he just witnessed God's great power and providence? Satan used Aaron's fear and desire. He frightened Aaron with thoughts that the people would become disgruntled and rebel; he enticed him with thoughts of the pleasure of being a popular, strong leader.

Moses, who had just returned from spending forty days basking in God's presence, couldn't be tempted at this point with any fear or pleasure because he knew the true happiness of communion with God—so he crushed the idol they had made to powder.

I hope that by now you've begun to identify the thoughts and desires that function as idols in your heart. Although they might seem godly, perhaps their prominence in your affections has made them idolatrous. Perhaps they are part of God's created order, but they've been distorted in some way; perhaps the world has told you that you can't be happy without them; or perhaps, like Aaron, you've been frightened or enticed to believe that a little idolatry, just in this case, is acceptable. But wherever these thoughts and desires have come from, if they've taken the place of God in your affections, they've got to go.

While you're identifying and watching against your false worship, you'll also need to identify the specific words and deeds that represent sinful patterns that flow out of the idolatry in your heart. Perhaps you are tempted to gossip, speak malicious words, be dishonest, or pout. Perhaps you become fearful or worried and shut down. Or you may give yourself over to sins of the flesh, such as gluttony, drunkenness, or sexual immorality. These patterns are the natural outgrowth of idolatry's law of diminishing returns. Idolatry never stands alone for long—it always breeds more and more sin. As you identify these patterns, you must through prayer and diligent effort seek to put these patterns to death.

Let me demonstrate how you might do this. Figure 11.1 is a form that I have completed in light of my problem with my friend we talked about in the previous chapter. (You'll find a blank copy of this form in Appendix A that you can copy and use.) Below are four questions that I've answered to help me understand how the sinful fruit grew out of idolizing my friend's opinion.

1. *Whom or what was I worshiping?* My friend's opinion and my self-righteousness.
2. *What did I want more than I wanted to be holy?* I wanted my friend to think well of me. I wanted to hear words of praise.

3. *What specific commandments did I ignore?* The first commandment, "Thou shalt have no other gods before Me" (Ex. 20:3 KJV); the second great commandment, because I didn't love my friend the way that I loved myself. I thought ill of her in defiance of Mark 12:31; I gossiped about her in defiance of 1 Timothy 3:11; I worried in defiance of Philippians 4:6; I was sinfully angry, ignoring Proverbs 29:8 and James 1:19–20.

4. *What specific sins do I need to put off? What should I put on?* I need to put off idolatry, self-love, self-righteousness, lack of love, gossip, and self-indulgence. I must put on the worship of God, love, right speech, humility, self-control, and proper confrontation.

Think now about the circumstance you considered in the last chapter, or pick a new one. What were the words you said, the actions you took? Did you slam doors or run to the refrigerator? Did you get on the phone and seek to commiserate with a friend? At every instance of a sinful thought, word, or deed, you must ask for God's grace to bring you to repentance while you seek to mortify or put off sinful behaviors and put on godly ones.

How should we treat the idols that we've found in our hearts? It's frightening that if we allow them one seemingly unimportant little place, their influence and power will grow and grow until they threaten to blot out our love for God. As Paul says, by the power of the Spirit we must put to death the deeds of the flesh (Rom. 8:13). We must kill them. We must burn them with fire and then crush them to powder. We can't cozy up with them or think that we can use them to help us get through until we get our spiritual act together. They're far too powerful for us to dally with. As Proverbs asks, "Can a man take fire in his bosom and his clothes not be burned?" (Prov. 6:27).

Fig. 11.1. Discovering Sinful Patterns and False Gods

	Monday	Tuesday	Wednesday	Thursday	Friday	Saturday	Sunday
Morning	Angry at friend for her criticism.				She called again and said the same things but also said she appreciated me.		Hoped that I didn't have to speak with her at church. Left in a hurry and slammed the car door.
Afternoon	Spoke with other friends about her ingratitude and ignorance.		Rehearsed in my mind all the things I'd like to say to her. Worried about what she thinks of me.		Fumed again about her criticism. Told her off in my mind. Remembered all the times she's criticized me in the past.		
Evening	Nagging thoughts of her words were the last thing that I thought of before falling asleep.	Worried about why I hadn't heard from her again. Wondered what she thought and became angry again.		Went out to dinner and overate because I felt sorry for myself. Decided that I would never help her again.			

Confession and Repentance

How do we kill idols? If we could see them, if they were solid pieces of silver or gold, we'd know what to do. We would pick them up and throw them out the nearest window. But these idols exist in our thoughts and imaginations. We know that they're there because they produce sinful words and behavior. How can we get rid of what seems to be an intrinsic part of who we are? We can take courage that God's Spirit, who searches hearts, is continually working to enlighten and enable us.

The assault against our idolatry and the sinful behavior that flows from it must begin on several fronts. The first battle will be fought on the field of prayer. Heartfelt, Spirit-led, and consistent confession and repentance is the only weapon that can weaken the strongholds that our idolatrous thoughts and desires occupy.

My husband and I enjoy learning about the Civil War. Whenever we travel, we love to find battlefields and tour them. For us, one of the most moving and fascinating battlegrounds is in Gettysburg, Pennsylvania. We may feel this way because one year we were blessed to arrive there on July 5, just in time to watch a reenactment of Pickett's charge. The battle on this particular day was pivotal because up until this point, the third day of fighting, it seemed as though the Confederates were going to win. But General Robert E. Lee underestimated the strength of his enemy's forces and ordered a brave but ill-fated charge across an open field into what he thought was the softest area of the enemy's line. Because the Union general, George Meade, held the high ground and was well entrenched, it didn't matter that thousands of men sincerely and bravely charged against his position. It held. In forty-five minutes, six thousand men lost their lives as wave upon wave of soldiers ran toward the "little copse of trees," trying to find the soft spot in the Federal defenses. They fell before the cannon and rifle fire before they could even reach Union lines. General Lee made a fatal mistake that day: he underestimated his enemy's strength and was misinformed about his prospects for victory.

Heart-Humbling Prayer

General Lee was fully convinced that his troops were strong enough to take the enemy that day. He was brave and willing to take the risks necessary if he might turn the tide of the war on that fateful battleground. He didn't lack commitment or bravery. What he lacked was accurate information about the strength and tactics of his enemy. And many men that day paid what Abraham Lincoln called "the last full measure of their devotion" because of his error.

The story of Pickett's charge is meaningful because in some ways that's what it's like when we try to change without first using the weapon of heart-humbling prayer. We can throw every self-help book, every good intention, every new discipline program, and all our resolutions against our well-entrenched enemies, only to find ourselves bloodied, discouraged, and running for the hills. It is only in the power of the Spirit that we comprehend our enemy's strengths and find the wisdom to tear down and destroy our idols. The Spirit comes to the aid of those who humble themselves, recognizing their utter helplessness and crying out for His help in desperation.

Confession of our neediness and sin humbles naturally proud hearts. Even though it's difficult to humble yourself, remember God "resists the proud, but gives grace to the humble" (1 Peter 5:5 NKJV). When I sit before Him in self-satisfied pride, I am not seeking His strength. I must recognize that Satan, my enemy, is strong and well entrenched and that without the Spirit's aid, I'll fall just like George Pickett's troops did. It doesn't matter how much willpower I think I have or how strong I think I've gotten; without the

Spirit, I'm doomed to fail. It's only as I get a picture of my absolute neediness that His power is present to help and change me.

Putting on humble confession is the door that opens streams of grace to me. I know He'll give me His help when I bow before Him, confessing that I'm hopeless and helpless without it. "He who conceals his transgressions will not prosper, but he who confesses and forsakes them will find compassion." Augustine said, "Confession shuts the mouth of hell and opens the gates of paradise."[1]

Think about Rachel's response when she was confronted for stealing her father's idols. Did she confess her sin? No, she tried to cover it up (Gen. 31:34). Consider, in contrast, David's confession, "Against You, You only, I have sinned and done what is evil in Your sight, so that You are justified when You speak and blameless when You judge" (Ps. 51:4). True confession doesn't make excuses or try to cover up guilt. We confess our sins because sin is an affront to a holy God. In confession we're saying that we agree with God's assessment of our behavior. His appraisal of our behavior is right and holy. You must first see yourself as a sinner before you can know the comfort of a Savior.

How should you confess your sins? You should confess them as precisely as possible. Thinking back on the circumstance I've discussed, I might say, "Father, please forgive my sin in Jesus' name. Forgive me for having another god before You. Forgive me for desiring Jane's good opinion rather than Yours; for neglecting the great joy in unhindered fellowship with You. Forgive me for gossiping, being sinfully angry, worrying, and being self-righteous." Confession should include not only the outer sinful behavior but also the desires and thoughts that prompt the behavior. As my heart is humbled before my Father, He is always moved with great compassion and has promised to forgive my sin.

1. Augustine, quoted in Thomas Watson, *The Doctrine of Repentance* (Carlisle, PA: Banner of Truth Trust, 1994), 34.

Because of the good news of the gospel, I can rest in the truth that my Father's arms are always open to me and that His heart is always inclined to love and forgive. As part of my confession, I can even confess that insomuch as this sin has taught me, once again, how much I need a Savior and how much I've been given in Christ, it is a good. Not that sinning itself is a good—but as I see it and repent of it, even my sin, heinous as it is, will help to spur me to gratitude and heartfelt love for the Father who will never let me go.

Ardent Repentance

After confession comes repentance. Repentance is a grace of God's Spirit by which we, as sinners, are inwardly humbled and visibly reformed. True repentance involves a hatred for sin and a turning from it and from all self-salvation projects. As I look into my heart, I see that although I want to turn from my sin, frequently it's not because I hate it. It's usually because it's embarrassing or troublesome. I long to develop a heart that burns with true repentance—and in order to do that I must plead with my Father to give me a genuine abhorrence of my sin. It's only as I hate my sin that I'll have the desire to fight it.

Ezekiel told the Israelites to "repent and turn away from your idols and turn your faces away from all your abominations" (Ezek. 14:6). Repentance doesn't involve only confession—saying, "I'm sorry" or "Okay, you're right." Putting it on involves a desire to turn away from our former loyalties and a belief that God will continue to love us in the process. It involves belief in His ongoing love for me and repentance for thinking His love is like me: contingent.

Our repentance will never be perfect, but if it is sincere, God counts it as perfect for His Son's sake.[2] Repentance is sincere when

---

2. "Perfection is His endowment; sincerity is ours." Richard Baxter, *A Christian Directory* (Morgan, PA: Soli Deo Gloria Publications, 1996), 67.

we offer up all our dearest thoughts, imaginations, and desires to God and seek to turn from them as an offering to the Lord. Again, this repentance will never be perfect or even perfectly sincere, but in faith we are to offer our desires to our Father who knows our hearts and remembers that we are dust.

Hungering and Thirsting for Righteousness

Jesus taught us to take sin seriously. In fact, He taught that we should hate our sin so much that we would be willing to go without what seems necessary for life. Are you willing to tear out your right eye or cut off your right hand in your struggle against idolatry? How much are you willing to give up to serve God? Are you willing to pay that "last full measure of devotion"? King David said that he was not willing to offer a sacrifice to the Lord that "cost [him] nothing" (2 Sam. 24:24).

Kay Arthur tells the story of a Pastor Hsi, who was brought to Christ under the ministry of Hudson Taylor in China. Hsi was an opium addict who, upon his conversion, knew that he must give up his habit. After days of fighting and warring with Satan's temptations, which included the fear of pain or death and the pleasure that just one puff of opium would bring, he said, "'Devil, what can you do against me? My life is in the hands of God. And truly I am willing to break off opium and die, but not willing to continue in sin and live.' In the moments of his greatest suffering he would frequently groan out loud: 'Though I die, I will never touch it again!'"[3] That's the kind of repentance that you'll need to put on in order to begin to crush your idols. This struggle is fierce because your idols and the sins that flow from them bring

---

3. Kay Arthur, *Lord, Only You Can Change Me* (Sisters, OR: Multnomah, 1995), 141.

you pleasure—perhaps as much pleasure as Hsi experienced at his opium pipe—and these pleasures calm the fears that have sunk their claws so deeply into your heart. You must be able to say with Hsi, "I might die in this struggle, but I'm not willing to continue in sin and live."

Jesus talked about this kind of desire for holiness.

> If your right eye makes you stumble, tear it out and throw it from you. . . . If your right hand makes you stumble, cut it off and throw it from you. (Matt. 5:29–30)

The sins that are dearest to us are the ones that we must pluck out and cast from us. We must deprive ourselves of all the desires that are most charming and profitable to us, however harmless they may seem, if we discover that they cause us to worship any other god or sin against Him. As Isaac Watts wrote in 1707, "All the vain things that charm me most, I sacrifice them through His blood."[4] These "vain things" are the delights that we hold most closely and that become our gods most easily.

What are you willing to give up to become holy? What cherished thoughts and desires are you ready to lay down on the altar of His grace? What would you sacrifice to know Him, to be conformed to His image, and to experience the fellowship of His sufferings?

Your Charming Gods

After we've confessed and repented of our sin and idolatry, we must turn from them and seek to put them to death. As in every facet of our progressive sanctification, we can do this only by the

---

4. Isaac Watts, "When I Survey the Wondrous Cross," 1707.

power of the Holy Spirit and by faith in the grace of the gospel. We must turn from our idolatry and sin, even if, at the beginning, that means stopping ourselves even in the midst of the act. Even if you've started to gossip, you can stop and say, "I shouldn't be talking like this. Will you please forgive me?" and then change the subject. If you find that you've exaggerated while telling a story, you could stop and say, "Please forgive me. I've just lied to you, and I don't want to sin against God in that way. This is what really happened . . ."

"Wow!" you might be thinking. "Doing that kind of thing will be too embarrassing . . . too painful!" Can you see why Jesus said that overcoming the sins that entrap us is like plucking out our eye or cutting off a hand?

Sometimes overcoming idolatry means that we have to change the place where we work or the relationships we allow, cut up our credit cards, or disconnect the television or Internet. We have to guard against the beginnings of sin. Perhaps we'll have to change the route we take to get home or refuse to renew season tickets to a beloved activity. Wherever we see idols flourishing, we'll need to turn away from not only the sin but also the occasion of it. Once again, it's not that some of these things might not be legitimate pleasures. The question is not whether they are legitimate, but whether we are entangled and enticed by them.[5]

You can't accomplish any lasting change on your own. It's the power of the Holy Spirit that accomplishes change. That's why Paul said that we must put to death the deeds of the flesh by the power of the Holy Spirit (Rom. 8:13). He's the only One strong enough to turn us from sin toward God.

---

5. "All things are lawful for me, but not all things are profitable. All things are lawful for me, but I will not be mastered by anything" (1 Cor. 6:12); "All things are lawful, but not all things are profitable. All things are lawful, but not all things edify" (1 Cor. 10:23).

Putting on Obedience

Progressive sanctification is a threefold process: putting off, the renewing of the attitude by belief in the good news, and putting on. Our holy worship includes obedience and heartfelt praise. We've already looked at why we're tempted to worship as we do and how to crush our idols by putting on confession and repentance. Now let's think about how to put on the holy worship that we long for.

Whenever the Bible teaches you to put off any sinful activity, it will always tell you what to put on in its place. You'll find some simple examples in figure 11.2 that demonstrate this principle.

Fig. 11.2. Scriptural Examples of the Putting Off/On Principle

Put Off	Put On
Anger	Humility, communication, and service (Eph. 4:26, 31–32)
Fear	Fear of God and love for others (Luke 12:4–5; 1 John 4:18)
Stealing	Hard work and giving (Eph. 4:28)
Hurtful Words	Kind, grace-filled words that build up (Eph. 4:29)
Worry	Thankful, specific prayer and disciplined thoughts (Phil. 4:6–9)

In the footnote is a list of references you can use to discover what further actions to put on.[6]

Let me illustrate this process with one example. Mary was a

6. Here is a partial list of put off/on injunctions: adultery (Prov. 5:15–23); anger (Eph. 4:26–32); change (Rom. 6; 12; 13:14; Gal. 5:19–23; 1 Peter 2:11–12); depression (Pss. 32, 38, 51); drunkenness (Eph. 5:18); evil communication (Eph. 4:25–32); envy (James 3:13–18); fear (Matt. 10:26–31; 1 John 4:18); love (1 Cor. 13; Col. 3:5–17); lying (Eph. 4:25); self-denial (Luke 9:23–24); trials (James 1); worry (Matt. 6:25–34; Phil. 4:6–9).

woman who struggled with many fears, the greatest being driving. Although she had two daughters who needed her to take them to their after-school sports and social clubs, she refused to drive on the freeway and drove very slowly, with the result that her girls were always late. Because of her tardiness, they were frequently unable to participate in games and activities. Mary knew that her fear was wrong but didn't know why or how she could overcome it.

Fig. 11.3. Specific Examples of the Putting Off/On Principle

Put Off	Renewed Thoughts	Put On	Specific Actions
The fear of driving caused by sinful imaginations and the desire to protect herself.	Meditation on God's promise to protect and keep her and the desire to please and glorify Him.	Repentance and confession. Faithful love for God and her daughters that eclipses her fear of calamity. Praise and worship.	Start driving small increments on the freeway. Occupy her thoughts with God's goodness by listening to worship music while driving.

Mary began the first step of progressive sanctification in this area when she saw that her fears were sinful. She had allowed her imagination to captivate her heart with thoughts of calamity. She wasn't keeping her thoughts focused on God's goodness and love for her. This fear had a great place in her because the desire that ruled her heart was self-protection. She confessed her fear and her sinful desire to protect herself to the Lord. Then she began to renew her mind by studying Scripture about God's fatherly care and His promises to keep her and love her because of Jesus' work on her behalf. But that wasn't enough. Mary needed to begin to put on godly actions. As she studied 1 John 4:18, "perfect love casts out fear," and learned that because of God's gracious salvation she didn't need to fear punishment or death, she began to understand that she needed to love her daughters more than she feared an accident. This love would provide the power to overcome fear. She began to take short trips on the freeway out of love for her daughters, all the while filling her mind with songs of praise for God's love. As time went on, she was able to drive further and further distances and soon found that driving, though difficult, was just another opportunity to rejoice in God's goodness to her.

Although this process seems simple, it is not simplistic. It is simple enough that children can learn it, yet it is so deep that God uses it to change the heart. As you wrestle with this process, please remember that it is just that: a process. Again, you may refer to the list of *put-offs* and *put-ons* in figure 11.2 (and in footnote 6) or you can do more investigation on your own.[7]

Don't Give Up

In this process of sanctification we'll have to resist the desire to give up and feel overwhelmed or to despair when we see our sin. Recognize that it's God's kindness that brings us to repentance. If God has kindly shown us our sin, then His love is strong enough to transform us and hang on to us in spite of the fact that we seem to be such easy prey to sinful lusts. As one Puritan put it, "Shall pardoned sins drive us from Him that pardons them?"[8]

---

7. You can find a more detailed explanation of the process of sanctification and specific *put-offs* and *put-ons* in the following books: Jay E. Adams, *The Christian Counselor's Manual* (Zondervan), *The Christian Counselor's New Testament* (Timeless Texts), *Competent to Counsel* (Zondervan); Wayne Mack, *A Homework Manual for Biblical Living: Personal and Interpersonal Problems* and *A Homework Manual for Biblical Counseling: Family and Marital Problems* (P&R); John MacArthur and Wayne Mack, *Introduction to Biblical Counseling* (W Publishing). Resources for Changing Lives from the Christian Counseling and Educational Foundation has a number of excellent booklets on specific topics, which are available from P&R Publishing or www.ccef.org.

8. Richard Baxter, *A Christian Directory* (Morgan, PA: Soli Deo Gloria Publications, 1996), 66.

Even though this seems like a difficult battle (and it is), you must ask yourself, "Are humiliation, confession, restitution, mortification, and holy diligence worse than hell?"[9] These are the stakes for which we are striving. We can have hope even in the face of our continuous failure that "the Lord knows how to rescue the godly from temptation" (2 Peter 2:9). God knows how to help you. The Lord Jesus has gone before you. He has purchased your freedom, cleansed your heart and conscience, empowered you with His Spirit, secured your soul in His hand. He can deliver you from your sin. Rest and rejoice in Him.

In this great grace that's been given to us, it is still our responsibility to diligently seek the Holy Spirit's guidance, to avail ourselves of every means of grace, especially the sacraments and the Word preached. We must put on directed energies to struggle against sin.

May We Not Crave Evil Things

Paul taught the Corinthians that the history recorded in Exodus is more than an interesting tale. He wrote,

> Now these things happened as examples for us, so that we would not crave evil things as they also craved. Do not be idolaters, as some of them were; as it is written, "The people sat down to eat and drink, and stood up to play." . . . Therefore, my beloved, flee from idolatry. (1 Cor. 10:6–7, 14)

As Paul reflected on Israel's idolatry, he discerned that all God's children, at all times, have a propensity to turn in their hearts away from the Lord. He desired that we would learn from Israel's sin,

---

9. Ibid., 90.

that we would think deeply about it and how we're like them. He understood that "men must have an object [to worship], and when he turns from the true God, he at once craves a false one."[10] It's so vital for us to keep our hearts stayed on Christ—to recognize that though He's absent from us here on earth, our Father is watching over us, protecting, pardoning, and leading us.

To my sadness, I've frequently heard Christian women say, "I know that Jesus is here with me . . . but I need something more. I need a god with skin that I can feel." I understand the struggle that we sometimes experience having to live our lives by faith, waiting for the return of our heavenly Husband, Jesus Christ, but when I hear this I'm so saddened. I'm reminded of the idolatry at the foot of the mountain thousands of years ago.

> They made a calf in Horeb
> And worshiped a molten image.
> Thus they exchanged their glory
> For the image of an ox that eats grass.
> They forgot God their Savior,
> Who had done great things in Egypt,
> Wonders in the land of Ham
> And awesome things by the Red Sea.
> Therefore He said that He would destroy them,
> Had not Moses His chosen one stood in the breach before Him,
> To turn away His wrath from destroying them. (Psalm 106:19–23)

Moses commanded all those who were on the Lord's side to put to death their neighbors who were idolaters. That's how serious this matter of idolatry is: you've got to be willing to annihilate it in your heart. It is the very sin of idolatry, self-salvation,

10. Arthur W. Pink, *Gleanings in Exodus* (Chicago: Moody Press, 1972), 316.

self-justification, and unbelief that annihilated your Savior on the Roman cross. You've got to look with disdain upon those "vain things that charm you most" and strap on the sword of the Spirit. You've got to put on daily belief in God's goodness and respond in confession, repentance, and a desire for obedience.

Have you forgotten your Savior's goodness? Have you forgotten how He did great things in delivering you from the hand of your enemy? If so, you can run to your kind Intercessor, Jesus Christ, who is standing in the breach before His Father, who has turned His just wrath away from you. By faith you can deal with the idolatry you see in your life—by His power and in His name He will enable you to slay your idols and put away all your false gods. Oh, and by the way, you do have a God with skin. His name is Jesus, the Incarnate Son.

FOR FURTHER THOUGHT

1. Thomas Watson wrote, "In Adam we all suffered shipwreck, and repentance is the only plank left us after shipwreck to swim to heaven."[11] What do you think he meant?

2. What steps must we take to begin to put off our sins and put on holiness?

3. Write out a prayer of humble confession.

4. Why is confession so important?

5. What specific steps should you take to repent of your idolatry?

11. Ibid., 13.

6. Are you aware of any actions you should take to pluck out your eye or cut off your hand? What are they? How important is it to you to grow in holiness? What are you willing to sacrifice?

7. How would remembering God's immutable love for you in Christ give you the courage and faith to continue to confess and repent? How does the gospel enable you to be both transparent and humble?

8. After reflecting on a particular besetting sin, fill in the table below. If you don't know what action to "put on," refer to footnote 6.

Fig. 11.4. Personal Worksheet for Putting Off and Putting On

Put Off	Renewed Thoughts	Put On	Specific Actions

9. Some Christians teach that repentance and confession should occur only as a first step in regeneration. The church father Tertullian thought he was born for no other end but to repent. What do you think? Why?

12

Delighting in God

An act of worship is vain and futile when
it does not come from the heart.[1]

When David brought the ark of God back to Jerusalem after it
had been taken by the Philistines, he did so with great passion and
joy. Although his first attempt ended in tragedy, with the death of
his friend (2 Sam. 6:5–7), David thrilled at the thought of God's
presence returning to Israel:

> David was dancing before the LORD with all his might. . . . So
> David and all . . . Israel were bringing up the ark of the LORD
> with shouting and the sound of the trumpet. . . . [Then Michal]
> saw King David leaping and dancing before the LORD. (2 Sam.
> 6:14–16)

King David, a man after God's own heart (1 Sam. 13:14),
danced before the Lord with everything that was in him. He
treasured the nearness of God's presence, and his great joy was
expressed through his actions. He was filled with "the highest ex-
pressions of joy that could be: He danced before the Lord with all
his might; he leaped for joy. . . . It was a natural expression of his

1. John Piper, *Desiring God: Meditations of a Christian Hedonist* (Sisters, OR: Multnomah,
1996), 79.

great joy and exultation of mind."[2] David was filled with glee and pleasure because he and his nation would again know the nearness of God.

I was recently reminded about Malachi's prophecy to those who would fear (worship and hold in awe) God's name. He said, "You will go forth and skip about like calves from the stall" (Mal. 4:2). I'm not a farm girl, so I've never seen a calf "skip about." I think I've seen this kind of behavior in my little Lhasa Apso. When she's released after being cooped up all day, she does laps around our yard at full speed. She seems so glad to get out of the house that her little legs simply explode with energy, and round and round she goes.

Have you ever been so moved by God's glory—His goodness, holiness, kindness, or mercy—that your heart just exploded with praise? Could you imagine being so taken up with God's majesty that you felt like dancing? David knew what it was to "skip about like a calf from the stall."

How long has it been since your heart "overflow[ed] with gratitude" (Col. 2:7)? That word *overflow* in Colossians means to superabound or excel with gratitude! What would it be like to burst forth with passionate praise . . . and why don't we? In answer to that question, A. W. Tozer writes,

> Orthodox Christianity has fallen to its present low estate from lack of spiritual desire. Among the many who profess the Christian faith scarcely one in a thousand reveals any passionate thirst for God. . . . We fear extremes and shy away from too much ardor in religion as if it were possible to have too

---

2. *Matthew Henry's Commentary on the Whole Bible: New Modern Edition*, electronic database (Peabody, MA: Hendrickson, 1991).

much love or too much faith or too much holiness. . . . [If you don't] refuse to surrender to the chill of your spiritual environment . . . you will reach at last (and unknown to you) the bone yard of orthodoxy and be doomed to live out your days in a spiritual state which can be best described as "the dead level and quintessence of every mediocrity."[3]

Impassioned Orthodoxy[4]

We have a God-given ability to enjoy and express emotion. Our passions can be excited by beauty; our emotions are moved by music, literature, and art; we can experience the depth of tragic sorrow and the height of ecstatic joy. He's created us with the ability to contemplate, comprehend (in a limited way), and enjoy Him, so that our hearts "overflow" with beautiful thoughts about our great King (Ps. 45:1). He's given us the ability to create, perform, and enjoy music and poetry in our worship, just so our hearts would be inclined more toward Him. Our ability to rejoice in God reflects His joy and exultation in Himself. Jesus Christ rejoices with all the saints in heaven over God's glory, "I will proclaim Your name to My brethren, in the midst of the congregation I will sing Your praise" (Heb. 2:12).

---

3. A. W. Tozer, *The Root of the Righteous* (Camp Hill, PA: Christian Publications, 1955), 56. Perhaps you're thinking, "Yes, Elyse, that's fine for people who are expressive or demonstrative . . . but I'm a quiet sort." That may be, but Edwards would answer you by saying that those who are moved in their affections because it's their personality or temperament have no assurance that they are being moved by God. If you're normally a staid and proper person and you are moved to superabound with gratefulness, you'll know that the Holy Spirit is at work in you! Are you the kind of person who relishes your proper, quiet demeanor? Think then that if God could move you to express joy and happiness at the apprehension of His grace toward you, what joy that would bring to Him whose goal it is to glorify Himself!

4. I first read this phrase in an article by Joshua Harris. According to him, the phrase *impassioned orthodoxy* originated with David Powlison of the Christian Counseling and Educational Foundation.

Do You Really Appreciate Your Adoption?

A couple I know recently adopted a baby girl, Katelyn. The couple who adopted her sought her out and brought her into their home with nothing (other than the fact that she needed parents) to recommend her. She was dependent on their mercy and love. Now, as their daughter, she's entitled to all of the privileges and blessings that will accrue to her as a member of that family.

Peter wrote that we who have been adopted are a "chosen race . . . a people for God's own possession . . . for you once were not a people, but now you are the people of God; you had not received mercy, but now you have received mercy" (1 Peter 2:9–10). God has brought us into His family, declared that we are His children, and given us all the rights and privileges that go along with sonship.

Right now Katelyn is unaware of the blessing that's become hers, but one day she'll rejoice in it. Her family will know she's maturing when she starts to express her thanks and gratitude for her parents' love. We, too, should exult in God's grace in adopting us into His family.

Why did God adopt us? Peter says that it is so we might "proclaim the excellencies of Him who has called you out of darkness into His marvelous light" (1 Peter 2:9). Do you realize that you've been called expressly for the purpose of proclaiming the excellencies of Christ? Does your heart overflow with praise for your Father's grace and kind condescension in adopting you? One way for you to know whether your heart is filled with this kind of praise is to listen to the words you speak. What do you praise? What kinds of words normally overflow your heart? It's hard to imagine that a heart is filled with praise if the mouth isn't busy proclaiming it. For "the mouth speaks out of that which fills the heart" (Matt. 12:34).

Is your heart filled with tender thoughts of God's goodness? Then your mouth will be also.

Let us be so taken up with the knowledge of God's goodness and grace that our emotions are warmed and our outer man (our mouth, our hands, our bodies)[5] reflect great love. Although we must not seek emotional experiences for their own sake, we must not shun them merely because others misuse them or ignore God's instructions on worship. How can we possibly put off the worship of other gods if we are not wholly taken up with the worship of the true God? Learning to take great delight and joy in God is the strongest deterrent to idolatry. Our hearts are only weaned from our idols by the power of a stronger love, the power of the Father's love for us in the gospel.

We play around with mud pies; we're lukewarm in our praise because we haven't tasted the sweet joy of communion with Him or we've forgotten what that joy was like when we first learned that Jesus was the friend of sinners. Jesus stood against the temptation to worship Satan because He knew the delight of His Father's smile. Part of overcoming idolatry involves growing in your grasp of the delight found in being loved by the most winsome Being in all creation.[6] "The most powerful worship will be among people whose minds linger in the light of truth and whose hearts—whose emotions—are as near the fire of God as they can be without being consumed."[7]

5. John Frame writes, "People communicate, not only by word, but also by body language. In this we image the God of Scripture, who communicates both through spoken word and through natural revelation. Some (especially Presbyterians like me) prefer to worship in a sitting position, but to most people in the world it is natural to accompany words with physical actions." John Frame, *Worship in Spirit and Truth: A Refreshing Study of the Principles and Practice of Biblical Worship* (Phillipsburg, NJ: P&R, 1996), 130–31.

6. Tozer refers to God as "the most winsome being in all creation." A. W. Tozer, *The Root of the Righteous* (Camp Hill, PA: Christian Publications, 1986), 15.

7. John Piper, *A Godward Life: Savoring the Supremacy of God in All of Life* (Sisters, OR: Multnomah, 1997), 69–70.

Praising Your God

Consider what the Puritans wrote about praise and holy affections:

> Alas, for that capital crime of the Lord's people—barrenness in praises! Oh, how fully I am persuaded that . . . an hour of praises is worth a day of fasting and mourning.[8]

> Praising God is one of the highest and purest acts of religion. In prayer we act like men; in praise we act like angels.[9]

> Self-love may lead us to prayers, but love to God excites us to praises.[10]

Whether you believe in singing psalms only, hymns only, or hymns and choruses, true worship must engage your body and your heart, which includes your mind, your affections, and your will. Our outer man, our body, should be engaged in some way: in speaking, singing, or shouting; standing, kneeling, or bowing (sitting is never the norm for worship in Scripture); with bowed or uplifted head, with uplifted or clapping hands. I recognize that mere outward postures are no guarantee against heartless worship (Mark 7:6–7), but Scripture invariably links bodily activity with hearts that are captivated by the glory of God.[11]

8. I. D. E. Thomas, comp., *A Puritan Golden Treasury* (Carlisle, PA: Banner of Truth Trust, 1997), 209, quoting John Livingstone.

9. Ibid., quoting Thomas Watson.

10. Ibid., quoting Thomas Manton.

11. Gen. 24:48; Ex. 15:20; Neh. 1:4; 8:6; 1 Chron. 29:20; Pss. 28:2; 30:11; 47:1; 63:4; 119:48; 134:1–2; 141:2; 149:3; 150:4; Lam. 3:40–41; 1 Tim. 2:8; Ezek. 44:15; Deut. 10:8; 18:7; Ezra 10:9. There are only a few instances of worshipers sitting before God, most of them in mourning and repentance. Only David is recorded as having sat before the Lord in prayer and worship (1 Chron. 17:16).

In *Desiring God*, John Piper writes that a true vision of God coupled with the animating power of the Holy Spirit will result in a warming of godly affections. He then writes that the "heat of our affections [produces] powerful worship, pushing its way out in confessions, longings, acclamations, tears, songs, shouts, bowed heads, lifted hands and obedient lives."[12]

Think about Piper's words again: powerful worship . . . *confessions, longings, acclamations, tears, songs, shouts, bowed heads, lifted hands, obedient lives*. Does your worship of God include these things? Think about the events that move your emotions and your body. Can you cheer with abandon at a football game or be moved to tears at a movie or laugh with great mirth at a play but find yourself unmoved before the King of the universe? Are you unmoved in your praise because you think that it is unsuitable to express emotion in worship? Do you believe that emotion is sinful per se? It is true that it can be. Zeal can be mixed with pride and passion and produce corruption. But does that mean that we should we shun zealous emotions altogether? Instead we must regulate and examine them. The questions we must ask include: Am I seeking after some emotional high for its own sake? Am I enjoying God in this worship, or am I merely enjoying a lifting of my emotions? Is it to God's majesty that I'm responding with zeal and passion? Biblical worship certainly seems to invoke zeal and emotions:

Bless the LORD, O my soul,
And all that is within me, bless His holy name. (Ps. 103:1)

My lips will shout for joy when I sing praises to You. (Ps. 71:23)

12. Piper, *Desiring God*, 77.

So I will bless You as long as I live;
I will lift up my hands in Your name

. . . .

My mouth offers praises with joyful lips. (Ps. 63:4–5)

You have turned for me my mourning into dancing;
You have loosed my sackcloth and girded me with gladness,
That my soul may sing praise to You and not be silent.
O Lord my God, I will give thanks to You forever.
    (Ps. 30:11–12)

The Lord is my strength and my shield;
My heart trusts in Him, and I am helped;
Therefore my heart exults,
And with my song I shall thank Him. (Ps. 28:7)

But let the righteous be glad; let them exult before God;
Yes, let them rejoice with gladness.
Sing to God, sing praises to His name;
Lift up a song for Him who rides through the deserts,
Whose name is the Lord, and exult before Him. (Ps. 68:3–4)[13]

I will rejoice greatly in the Lord,
My soul will exult in my God. (Isa. 61:10)[14]

These verses and many others command us to worship God in ways that express deep gratitude, longing for Him, and joy for our salvation and His measureless grace to sinners. This gratitude,

---

13. The word translated "exult" is ʿalats, which means "to jump for joy, i.e. exult" (Vine's).

14. The word translated "greatly rejoice" is suws, which means "to be bright, i.e. cheerful." The KJV translates it "be glad, greatly, joy, make mirth, rejoice." The word exult is giyl, which means "to spin round (under the influence of any violent emotion), i.e. usually rejoice" (Vine's).

longing, and joy should overflow our hearts, causing praise for His character and nature. We are not free to praise God in any way we decide; we are to worship Him in the ways that He has prescribed. God has told us how to praise Him. We are to do so with all that is within us, with shouts of joy, with songs of thanks and gladness, with faces and hands uplifted![15]

Should not we, who know the mercy of redemption, be filled with more praise than the angels who have worshiped since the beginning of time? God recounts how all the "morning stars sang together and all the sons of God shouted for joy" (Job 38:7). How much more should we, who have been forgiven, redeemed, adopted, and made heirs of His kingdom, praise Him and shout for joy? Indeed, the heavens are filled with praise (Rev. 19:5–7), and the inanimate is moved before Him (Isa. 6:4; Luke 19:40). This demonstrative worship is the environment of God. Heaven is filled with prayers and praises, and our eternity will be spent singing and rejoicing in His magnificence.[16]

Portraits of Our Hearts

In Southern California where I live, we have a marine layer or cloudiness known to the locals as June Gloom. The marine layer is a blanket of fog that hangs off our coast and moves inland from time to time, especially during the month of June when the tourists show up and wonder what happened to the sun. I'm sure a meteorologist could tell us the cause of this phenomenon, but most of the natives who live here couldn't. We just live with it.

For many people, that's how it is with their emotions. We experience fears, joys, sorrows, depressions, and angers without ever understanding the causes. To many it may seem as if these emotions

---

15. See John Frame, *Worship in Spirit and Truth*

16. Rev. 5:9–14; 11:15–17; 14:3; 15:3–4; Pss. 103:20–22; 148:11–13; 150:6.

roll in on some mornings and clear up at other times for no apparent reason. Although the ways in which we experience emotions do seem perplexing, they aren't so ambiguous. Simply put, emotions are mirrors of our hearts. Our emotions reveal our thoughts and intentions; they reveal the judgments we've made about our circumstances. Our fears, sorrows, or joys are the ways we vividly experience the results of our thoughts and desires. If you are experiencing a particular emotion, that's usually because you've harbored certain thoughts or desires in your heart that give rise to this feeling.[17] For instance, if you feel sad, it's usually because your thoughts or desires have been disappointed in some way. Your responses to the daily trials or blessings of life are the primary causes of the emotions you feel every day. If you feel like jumping for joy, again that's due to the fact that your thoughts and desires are pleased. Our feelings work in concert with our affections, our minds, our wills, our consciences.

Our emotions are not under our direct control but flow out from the heart. It's ridiculous to get up in the morning saying, "Today, I'm going to be very happy" or "Today, I'm going to be angry." That's because our emotions don't work that way. Our emotions respond to and reflect our inner thoughts, and it's only as we center these thoughts on God's goodness, kindness, and love that we find joyful praises springing up from our hearts. Are your emotions ever warmed by thoughts about God's majesty or His kindness and nearness to you? If your thoughts and desires are consumed with Him, your emotions will respond. If you never find yourself moved emotionally, then you must ask whether you are seeing Him as He has declared Himself to be: your loving Heavenly Father, your faithful Heavenly Bridegroom.

17. This is usually the case; however, there are times when our physiological state (e.g., hunger or exhaustion) can cause us to experience emotions the way that Elijah did after running from Ahab. It is true that he was fearful and thought that his life was going to be forfeit to Jezebel, but his exhaustion and hunger fed his depression and thoughts of death. God comforted him through rest, water, food, and eventually His Word.

Meditating on Him

Entering into joyful praise is a by-product of meditation on His mercy and grace, magnificence, holiness, justice, and kindness. "God is surely more glorified when we delight in His magnificence," writes Piper, "than when we are so unmoved by it we scarcely feel anything."[18] If you have trouble "delighting in His magnificence" or "overflowing with gratitude,"* perhaps it's because your thoughts and desires aren't occupied with Him. How frequently do you meditate on His mercy or goodness? If you long to engage your whole heart in worship, you can spark your emotions by meditating on His gracious love for you.[19] Meditating on His goodness is part of putting on pure worship.

Think with me now about God's grace in your life: Who is He to you? What has He done for you? How has He loved you? Paul's list of the believer's blessings in Ephesians 1:3–14 should move you so that your heart bursts with praise for all the blessings given to you in the gospel:

- He has blessed you with every spiritual blessing in the heavenly places in Christ.
- He has chosen you in Him before the foundation of the world.
- In Christ, He has made you holy and blameless before Him.
- In love, He predestined you for adoption as a son through Jesus Christ to Himself, according to the kind intention of His will, which He freely bestowed on you in the Beloved.

18. Piper, *Desiring God*, 86.
19. If you find it difficult, refer to the description in chap. 7, pages 122–123, of the characteristics of God. Each of those adjectives has Scripture references that you can look up.

- In Him, you have redemption through His blood, the forgiveness of your trespasses, according to the riches of His grace that He lavished on you.
- In all wisdom and insight, He made known to you the mystery of His will, according to His kind intention.
- In Him, you have obtained an inheritance.
- You were sealed in Him with the Holy Spirit of promise, who is given as a pledge of your inheritance.
- You have become God's dearly loved personal possession.

If you aren't moved by the preceding list, go back over it and in every place where the word *you* appears, insert the word *I, me,* or *my.* Can you feel the gladness and gratitude that Paul felt as he penned this exquisite passage? Do you know why God has done all these things for you? Paul tells us in verses 12 and 14, "the praise of His glory." To what end has God chosen, adopted, redeemed, forgiven, and enlightened you? So that you might burst forth with loving praise of His glory! Do you live to praise the glory of His grace, and does that praise flow forth from you?

Matthew Henry writes that "we should live and behave ourselves in such a manner that his rich grace might be magnified, and appear glorious, and worthy of the highest praise."[20] Another commentator writes that "the grand end of His predestination is that the glory of His grace may be praised by all His creatures."[21] Albert Barnes even goes on to say that "all" that is done by election is suited to excite praise.

God chooses people to be holy, not sinful; to be happy, not miserable; to be pure, not impure; to be saved, not to be lost.

---

20. *Matthew Henry's Commentary on the Whole Bible: New Modern Edition,* electronic database (Peabody, MA: Hendrickson, 1991).

21. *Jamieson, Faucet, and Brown Commentary* (electronic database; Seattle: Biblesoft, 1997).

For these things he should be praised. . . . Had he chosen but one to eternal life, that one should praise him, and all the holy universe should join in the praise. . . . How much more is praise due to Him, when the number chosen is not one, or a few, but when millions which no man can number, shall be found to be chosen to life.[22]

Do you see how gracious God has been to you? As you come to Him, rejoicing passionately in His graciousness toward you, you will experience the renewal of joy that only true worshipers have. Don't be afraid to rejoice in Him for what He has done. Don't foolishly think that He only wants you to rejoice because of who He is, detached from interaction with you. Who He is is known to us primarily by what He has done for us! Is He merciful? Is He loving? Is He filled with patience and forgiveness? How do you know?

John Calvin believed that passionate love and worship originate in understanding His benefits. "Piety is reverence joined with the love of God which the knowledge of His benefits induces . . . unless they establish their complete happiness in Him, they will never give themselves truly and sincerely to Him."[23] In other words, unless we know that our total happiness and joy is to be found in Him, we'll never come to Him with worship and obedience. We no longer need to justify ourselves or try to put on a good face. We've been completely justified. His salvation is to the uttermost. "To honor God in worship we must not seek Him disinterestedly," Piper writes, "for fear of gaining some joy in worship and so ruining the moral value of the act. But instead, we must seek Him the way a thirsty deer seeks the stream, precisely for the joy of seeing and knowing Him!"[24]

22. *Barnes Notes* (electronic database; Seattle: Biblesoft, 1997).

23. John Calvin, *Institutes of the Christian Religion*, ed., John T. McNeill, 2 vols., Library of Christian Classics (Philadelphia: Westminster, 1960), 1:41.

24. Piper, *Desiring God*, 87.

As you seek to put off idolatrous worship, replacing it with obedience, you'll need to put on a heart that appreciates, loves, rejoices in, and celebrates the beauty, kindness, holiness, and majesty of your King. All other gods and their faint promises will pale when compared with the greatness and glory of the Lord. A heart that is crammed with thoughts of God's beauty, kindness, holiness, majesty, glory, and grace has no room for feeble counterfeits and will inevitably burst forth with fervent praises.

Is your heart continually drawn to worship other gods? If so, could it be that your focus is on worldly joys and pleasures? Do you have a portrait of His grandeur and the blessing of communing with Him by His grace? Even when you fail? Especially when you fail? Remember that the Puritans, when defining the duties required under the first commandment, said that we must "worship and glorify Him by . . . adoring, loving, desiring . . . delighting and rejoicing in Him; being zealous for Him; giving Him all praise and thanks."[25] These words speak of both an intellectual and emotional response to His love. How can you give Him all praise and thanks if you don't have a heart that rejoices in His goodness and benefits? Don't be deceived: you are already passionately worshiping something. Like Adam, you have been created with a God-given capacity for worship—the only question that remains is its focus. God created Adam for His glory—so that His glory would be known through Adam's praise and worship.

You'll discover that your obedience will become more pleasant when your heart is focused on His love for you and your responsive love for Him. For instance, putting off anger becomes easier for me when I meditate on the kindnesses of the Lord. When I find myself tempted to sin by becoming angry, part of the process of putting

25. The Larger Catechism, Q. 104 (Carlisle, PA: Banner of Truth Trust, 1998).

on the right action is rehearsing His forgiveness and grace in song. You'll find obedience more enjoyable when it's joyful. Conversely, your worship will leap to flame when you remember how He has loved you and when you seek to respond to that love.

I'm not a poet, but I'm thankful for the gift of writing that some Christians have. I find in some hymns the words that my heart has thought, written in a way that causes my affections to blaze with love. When I'm struggling with my false gods, with the desires of the world that would captivate my heart, I'm comforted and strengthened by words like these:

> And can it be that I should gain
> An interest in the Savior's blood?
> Died He for me, who caused His pain—
> For me, who Him to death pursued?
> Amazing love! How can it be,
> That Thou, my God, shouldst die for me?
> Amazing love! How can it be,
> That Thou, my God, shouldst die for me?

> He left His Father's throne above
> So free, so infinite His grace—
> Emptied Himself of all but love,
> And bled for Adam's helpless race:
> 'Tis mercy all, immense and free,
> For O my God, it found out me!
> 'Tis mercy all, immense and free,
> For O my God, it found out me!

> Long my imprisoned spirit lay,
> Fast bound in sin and nature's night;

Thine eye diffused a quickening ray—
I woke, the dungeon flamed with light;
My chains fell off, my heart was free,
I rose, went forth, and followed Thee.
My chains fell off, my heart was free,
I rose, went forth, and followed Thee.

No condemnation now I dread;
Jesus, and all in Him, is mine;
Alive in Him, my living Head,
And clothed in righteousness divine,
Bold I approach th'eternal throne,
And claim the crown, through Christ my own.
Bold I approach th'eternal throne,
And claim the crown, through Christ my own.[26]

Putting on True Worship

In this chapter I've encouraged you to put on true worship. Aside from the joy that infects your praises, it should also move you to respond in grateful love for your neighbor.

God is seeking worshipers (John 4:23) because it is His plan to make us into those who know the exquisite joy of surrendered worship to, intense love for, admiring awe of, and astonished wonder at His person and presence. In our worship and His transforming power He is glorified, finds joy, and enables us to enjoy the pleasures He's granted us forever. He's committed Himself to transforming us from servile, fearful, angry idolaters to happy children, playing in the garden of His delights, all for His ultimate glory and our enjoyment. May we, in all that we do, seek to humbly submit

26. Charles Wesley, "And Can It Be?" (1738).

to His work and fervently worship Him, reflecting to Him and the world around us the excellence of His glorious grace.

FOR FURTHER THOUGHT

1. Review the following verses and note why and how God's children are commanded to worship: Psalms 7:17; 9:1–2; 21:13; 30:1–4; 33:1–3; 66:1–5; 146:2; 149:1–3.

2. Write out the words to a favorite hymn or praise chorus. In what ways does this song touch your heart? What are the phrases that speak to you and stir your emotions?

3. Write out a prayer that God would enliven your heart to holy affections and deliver you from all idols.

4. In four or five sentences, write out the primary truths you've learned in this study.

Appendix A

Discovering Sinful Patterns and False Gods

1. Whom am I worshiping? Who is functioning as my god?

2. What do I want more than I want to be holy?

3. What specific commandments have I ignored or disobeyed?

4. What specific sins do I need to put off? What should I put on in their place?

Appendix A. Discovering Sinful Patterns and False Gods

	Monday	Tuesday	Wednesday	Thursday	Friday	Saturday	Sunday
Morning							
Afternoon							
Evening							

Appendix B

What It Means to Be Legalistic

Practically every time the topic of the law is mentioned, someone will say, "We aren't under the law! Isn't it legalistic to try to obey it?" Since it seems to me that misconceptions about God's law abound, let me try to define what I believe it means to be legalistic. I believe that legalism is played out in two common ways.

Keeping the Law as a Means of Staying Saved

No true Christian believes that he can earn his salvation by keeping the law. Paul put this reality in this way, "For we maintain that a man is justified by faith apart from works of the Law" (Rom. 3:28). That's one of the hallmark differences between true and false Christianity. If you're required to add anything to Christ's righteousness to attain salvation, whether that's circumcision, baptism, or any other good work, then you're falling into the same error as the Galatians. Paul sought to combat this misconception when he wrote so forcefully, "You have been severed from Christ, you who are seeking to be justified by law; you have fallen from grace" (Gal. 5:4).

Although most Christians would heartily agree with the truth that we are justified by faith alone, many are tempted to believe that their continuance in salvation rests on their ability to keep the law once they are saved. In other words, we recognize that we can't do anything to get saved, but once we are saved, we think we are completely responsible to maintain our salvation by living a good life.

Falling into this error is possible only if we have a shallow view of our personal sinfulness and our utter inability to live righteously. It seems to me that it would be difficult for any person who was deeply acquainted with his own thorough wickedness to assume that his salvation rested at any moment on himself. In fact, the thought that our salvation, our continuance in God's favor, rested upon our ability to please and obey Him ought to be terrifying, unless we lower God's standards in some way.

It is due to the false belief that Christians are able to maintain their salvation through good works that people fall into legalistic ways of thinking and acting. So, whereas a true Christian would never say that his justification or standing before God depends on himself, he might be tempted to say that his perseverance in the faith rests on his ability to stay saved. Once again, Paul fought this error in the Galatian church:

> Are you so foolish? Having begun by the Spirit, are you now being perfected by the flesh? . . . So then, does He who provides you with the Spirit and works miracles among you, do it by the works of the Law, or by hearing with faith? (Gal. 3:3, 5)

I'm not saying that we shouldn't be concerned about doing good works or seeking to obey the law. What I am saying is that our good standing before Him doesn't rest upon our ability to perform. Just as our first step in salvation, justification, rests solely on Christ and His righteousness, so do all of our successive steps. We are not able to keep ourselves from falling utterly, but He is: "Now to Him who is able to keep you from stumbling, and to make you stand in the presence of His glory blameless with great joy . . ." (Jude 24). Paul encouraged Timothy to rest in the knowledge of God's power to keep him, "for I know whom I have believed and I am convinced that He is able to guard what I have entrusted to Him until that day" (2 Tim. 1:12).

Our confidence should not rest in our power to do what we think pleases Him. Because of Christ, we already please Him. And when it comes to our ongoing sanctification, we can rest in the power of God, as Paul wrote, "For I am confident of this very thing, that He who began a good work in you will perfect it until the day of Christ Jesus" (Phil. 1:6). The further we stray from this truth, the more we will find ourselves mired in miserable, joyless legalism until we finally give ourselves up to indifference or self-indulgence for a time.

Adding to the Law

In a closely related area, legalism is lived out when people add to the standards that God has set. Let me give you an example of how this might be done. We all agree that God commands us to pray every day. That command is nonnegotiable. I believe it—I want to obey it. But how I handle the command to pray is open to my discretion.

For instance, I can rightly say that it is wise for me personally to get up at 6:00 a.m. every day so I'll have time to pray. That's not legalism; that's a reflection of my desire to spend time with the Lord before my day comes crashing in on me. In doing so, I trust that God will continue to produce the fruit of the Spirit, self-discipline, in my life so that I can attain my goal of consistent prayer and, in the process, obey the Lord.

It would be legalism, however, for me to tell you that God commands you to get up at 6:00 a.m. to pray. By doing that, I would be adding to what God has commanded. I can recommend that you get up early to pray, I can testify about my success in doing so, but I can't command you or tell you that God is commanding you to do so. This would be equivalent to adding to God's law. It's disturbing to realize that adding to God's law is analogous to saying that we know more than God about personal holiness and that He needs our help. We can see how silly that would be, but we frequently do it anyway.

This kind of legalism plays out in many ways, especially in outward conformity to manmade standards such as dressing in certain ways and avoiding certain places or types of entertainment. It is characterized in the old saw, "I don't smoke or chew, or run with them that do." It isn't that we shouldn't be concerned about our obedience to God's laws. The error lies in believing that our right standing before God rests upon obedience to our personal standards.

Paul was confronting this problem as it was displayed in the issue of eating meat sacrificed to idols when he said, "The faith which you have, have as your own conviction before God" (Rom. 14:22). Paul wasn't saying that you could make up anything you fancied regarding the doctrines of the faith. He was saying that in the realm of your personal liberty or conscience, be careful that you don't place your standards, your personal preferences and choices, on par with the Lord's—His are high enough.

In summary, legalism is lived out when we think that we must keep God's commands to ensure our ongoing salvation or when we place our personal convictions or means of obedience on par with His flawless commands.

Appendix C

How You Can Know
If You Are a Christian

I'm so glad that you decided to turn to this page, way in the back of this book—and there are two reasons why I feel this way.

First of all, the truths that are contained in this book will be impossible for you to understand and follow if you aren't a Christian, and I want you to be able to know the joy of God-empowered change. But that isn't the most important reason that I'm glad that you decided to turn here.

I'm also so pleased that you turned to this page because I long for you to know the joy of peace with God and to have the assurance that your sins are forgiven. If you've never come to the place in your life where God opened your heart to the truth of His great love and sacrifice and your rebelliousness and need for forgiveness, you must question whether you are a Christian.

Many people attend church or try to live good lives. We aren't as bad as we could be . . . and so we think that like Patrick Swayze's character in *Ghost*, it doesn't matter if we have trusted in Christ—if we're nice and we love people, God will accept us . . . right? If it were up to me, if you had to live up to my standards, I might say that we're all okay. But that's not the truth, and it isn't up to me. It's up to God . . . and His standards are different from mine. He says, "My thoughts are not your thoughts, nor are your ways My ways" (Isa. 55:8).

The truth is that God is perfectly holy. That means that He never thinks or does anything that is inconsistent with His perfection. He is pure and without fault of any kind. That's not because He gets up every morning and says, "I'll try to be good today." By His nature He is good, and there's never a time when He isn't.

In addition to being perfectly holy, He is just. That means that He always sees that justice is served—that those who deserve punishment always receive it in the end. It may not seem that way to you, looking at things as we do from an earthly perspective, but let me assure you, the great Judge of all the earth will prevail. If God allowed people to get away with breaking His laws, then He wouldn't be holy, would He?

In one sense, the truth of God's holiness and justice reassures us. The Hitlers of the world, even though they seemingly have escaped judgment on earth, will stand before their Creator and will receive what they deserve. But, in another sense, God's holiness and justice should make us all uncomfortable. That's because, even though we may not be as bad as we could be, we know that we all sin, and God hates sin. Sin is any violation of God's perfect standards. His standards are contained in the Bible and were summed up in the Ten Commandments in the Old Testament. Think for a moment about those commandments. Have you had any other gods in your life? Have you reverenced the Lord's Day and set it apart for Him? Have you always honored those in authority over you? Have you ever taken another's life or turned your back on someone who needed your protection? Have you ever desired someone who was not your spouse? Have you ever taken anything that wasn't yours to take? Have you ever told a lie or looked at something that someone else had and wanted it for yourself?

I'm sure, if you're like me, you'll say that you've probably broken each of God's commands at some time in your life. That means that there will come a time when you, too, will stand before

God's judgment seat. But don't despair. If you know that you are a sinner, then there is hope for you, because God is not only holy and just—He's also merciful.

God has mercy and pity on His people. He has immense love, and because of this, He made a way for you and me to come to Him. He did this without compromising His holiness and justice. Someone had to take the punishment for your sin. Someone had to die in your place. But who could do this and still maintain God's justice?

Every person who had ever lived sinned and was therefore disqualified from taking someone else's punishment, because they deserved punishment of their own. Only one Man could take this punishment. Only one Man was perfectly sinless and completely undeserving of punishment. That Man was Jesus Christ. Jesus Christ was God (making Him perfectly sinless) and man (making Him suitable as our stand-in). The Bible teaches that because of God's love for man, He sent His Son, Jesus Christ, to die in our place. On the cross, Jesus Christ took the punishment we deserved. Thus is God's justice served and His holiness upheld. That's why the Bible teaches that "while we were yet sinners, Christ died for us" (Rom. 5:8).

But that still leaves you with a problem. Perhaps as you are reading this you know that you are a sinner. You also believe that God is holy and just, and you are hoping that He is as merciful and loving as I've portrayed Him. What must you do? You must believe on Him. That means that you must believe what I've written and you must ask God to forgive you of all your sins. You can do this through prayer. There aren't any special words that you must say. In fact, the Bible says that "whoever will call on the name of the Lord will be saved" (Rom. 10:13). You can pray to Him, asking Him to forgive your sin because of Jesus' sacrifice. You can ask Him to make you His own. The Bible says, "If we confess our sins, He is faithful and righteous to forgive us our sins and to cleanse us from all unrighteousness" (1 John 1:9). You can rest in His truthfulness.

If you have become a Christian, you will want to live for Him in a way that pleases Him. In order to know how to do that, you must begin reading His Word. I recommend you begin in the Gospel of John with the first chapter. As you read, pray that God will help you to understand. The next thing that you should do is find a good, Bible-believing church and start attending it. A Bible-believing church is one that believes in the Trinity (that the Father, the Son, and the Holy Spirit are equally one God), believes that salvation is entirely a free gift of God, practices prayer and holiness, and preaches from God's Word without any other books added.

If you've become a Christian through the ministry of this book, I would love to know so that I can rejoice with you. Please write to me through my website: www.elysefitzpatrick.com. May God's richest blessings be yours as you bow humbly before His throne.